Also by Alissa Grosso

Shallow Pond
Ferocity Summer
Popular

How to Make Money *Selling Vintage Items on Etsy:*

Open a Store, Find Inventory, Take Photos, Create Listings, and Make Money Selling Vintage Items in This Billion-Dollar Marketplace

Alissa Grosso

ADVENTURE CONTINUES PRESS
2016

© 2016 Alissa Grosso
All rights reserved.

ISBN: **978-1535171373**
ISBN 13: **1535171375**

Contents

Introduction	1
Chapter 1: Getting Started	5
Chapter 2: Finding Inventory	15
Chapter 3: What to Sell	31
Chapter 4: Listing Items	85
Chapter 5: Shipping	117
Chapter 6: Marketing	143
Chapter 7: Customer Service	159
Chapter 8: Etsy Tools and Tricks	167
Chapter 9: Business Basics	183
Chapter 10: Cleaning House & Dealing with Duds	191
Chapter 11: Selling Beyond Etsy	201
Final Thoughts	215
Resources	217

Introduction

It's Sunday morning, and I'm driving over to the local high school track to run some laps when a Sale 2-Day sign and what, at first glance, appears to be a pile of rusty old junk catches my eye. I put my blinker on and maneuver into a vague sort of parking spot on the shoulder of the road. The track can wait.

The place is a mishmash of stuff. There are old things, new things, camping gear—and it's all over the place. There's stuff arranged at the front of the property, and then there's stuff down and around back outside. Plus, there's more in two different rooms in the house. It's my least favorite kind of sale in that nothing is priced. I like to know when I pick something up just what the owner is expecting to get for it. I've learned that some people have unreasonable expectations. Judging by all the older items and the age of the guy running the sale, this is someone who is a bit of a collector or perhaps a dealer. All the same, I pick up a few items. By the time I've completed my tour of the property, I have five items in my hands. It's not a windfall, but based on the lack of pricing, I'm trying to be conservative.

When I bring my stash back out front to the man running the sale and ask him what I owe him, he says, "My first estimate would be about twenty-five dollars." I don't say anything, but he must see the look in my eyes that says "too high," because almost immediately he says, "But how about we make it twenty?"

"Twenty I can do," I say, and I fork over my cash and head off to the track. As I get back on the road, I start to second-guess myself. Why did I spend so much money on a few measly items? Then I consider the items I bought. I decide I only need to sell a couple of them to make back my investment. I'll be fine.

Later, after my shower and lunch, the light's about right for snapping some pictures of my new treasures, as well as the items I bought on Saturday while hitting up a few garage sales. I clean up the items and then get to work with my camera. I upload the pictures and then get to putting up some Etsy listings. One of the items I list is an old, metal, hard-sided wallet that was one of the five items I bought on the way to my run. After some quick research, I list it at thirty dollars.

That evening, an e-mail comes through with the message that the wallet has sold, and I'm pleased because I know I didn't pay too much this morning.

This is what I love about Etsy. How cool is it to be able to buy an item in the morning and sell it mere hours later to someone somewhere else in the country, earning some money along the way?

Etsy is one of the easiest and most enjoyable ways I've found to make money online, and what's cool is that pretty much anyone can do it. You won't even need a lot of capital to get started with your Etsy shop. In fact, if you're like me, you could probably get started by cleaning out your attic or offloading some items you've had but don't necessarily need anymore.

I sold my first vintage item on Etsy in February of 2010, though I didn't really get serious about my vintage Etsy shop until the fall of 2011. Since then, I've sold over two thousand items on Etsy.

It's not my sole source of income, but it does bring in a steady amount of money that I've come to rely on. In this guide, I'll share what I've learned about running a vintage shop on Etsy, with tips on how you can start your own shop, find items to sell, and start making money.

Chapter 1
Getting Started

Etsy Basics

Etsy is an online marketplace initially started by artists as a place to sell their work and products online. The site has grown to include all manner of handcrafted items, as well as supplies for making those crafts. At this time Etsy offers sellers the opportunity to list products that fall into three main categories: Handmade, Supplies, and Vintage.

This book focuses on selling vintage items on Etsy, though as a seller you may also want to include handcrafted or supplies as part of your store inventory or even to open other stores that offer products in these categories. Vintage, as Etsy defines it, is any item that is at least twenty years old. If it's not at least twenty years old, or you didn't make it yourself, or it's not some sort of supply for making an item, then you cannot sell it on Etsy.

The good news is that there are a lot of items out there that fall into the vintage category. You'll find them at thrift stores, at auctions, at rummage sales, at yard sales, and, most likely, in your own home as well. Of course, not every item that's at least twenty years old has value, but a lot of them do, and determining the sort of items that will do well on Etsy can be as simple as browsing the vintage items currently posted for sale in the Etsy marketplace or reading through the "What To Sell" chapter of this book.

In order to sell on Etsy, you will need to set up your Etsy store. Etsy uses a storefront style for its sellers, which means if you only plan on selling a handful of items at a time, the Etsy marketplace may not be the best fit for your business model. But if you have or plan on acquiring a larger inventory, then Etsy will likely work well for you. There is no fee to open a store on Etsy. Instead, Etsy charges you twenty cents to list an item for four months (or until it sells) and charges a 3.5 percent transaction fee for each sold item. Depending on the payment method a buyer chooses, there may be an additional transaction fee. Buyers can pay with their PayPal accounts or via a credit card; both methods involve a small transaction fee. You have the option of accepting payments by mail as well, though most online shoppers are not interested in this slower method of payment, and for some sellers, having to deal with paper payments simply isn't worth it.

Before creating a shop, you will need to create an Etsy account if you don't already have one. The Etsy username you select cannot be changed; this will link to your public profile and can be the same as the shop name you select, but it does not need to be. No matter how many shops you have on Etsy, you will have a single public profile. This will include a short description about who you are, where you live (you can be as specific or as general as you care to be), and a small image. The image can be a personal photo of you, a logo, an item from your shop, or any other appropriately representative image. This is the equivalent of the profile picture for Facebook users, although folks on Etsy tend not to change them as much as Facebookers do.

In order to set up a shop on Etsy, you will first need to determine a name for your shop. Shop names can be changed, but it's a good idea to spend some time thinking about a name that best represents who you are and what you sell. Keep in mind that if the shop name you select is already in use, you will need to come up with a different name. So try to be unique in selecting a name for your store.

Once you've settled on a name, you will need to upload an image to use as the banner or header for your shop. Although you can opt to not include any image, this will help you with branding your shop, and it will help to make your shop's name stand out to Etsy shoppers. This will appear above your listings on your shop page whether shoppers are using a web browser on a computer or a mobile device. Take note of the size requirements and use either your computer's own built-in image editing software or an online image editor (I find the free Picmonkey.com very easy to use) to size your image accordingly. A free online editing tool called Canva offers an Etsy banner template that is free to use and customize. This image should include in text the name of your shop and can be a combination of text and images or text only, depending on your own style and preferences. Like your shop name, you are free to change this image at any time.

Etsy makes a point of emphasizing that their website is composed of individuals who make or resell products and takes great strides to emphasize the independent, noncorporate nature of their sellers. For that reason, shop owners are encouraged to introduce themselves to their buyers on the "About" page of their shops using a combination of text and images. While you may be eager to get your shop up and running and start selling, you don't want to skip this step. It's a great way to let potential buyers know who you are so they can feel comfortable buying from you.

Other things you might want to set up before you list items are your store sections and your shipping profiles. While you don't need to do these before you start selling, it might make it easier for you when you sit down to list your first items.

Shop sections give you a way to organize the items that you sell and make it easy for browsing buyers to locate items. If you have only a few items in your shop, these categories may not seem necessary, but as your shop grows to a hundred items or more, the sections will go a long way toward keeping things organized and findable. Your shop needs to be open to the public in order to add shop sections—that is, if you have vacation settings turned on, you will not be able to do this. You can add up to fifteen shop sections. The sections that you choose will depend on what sort of items you are or will be selling and what you think will make the most sense for shoppers. You are free to change these sections at any time.

Shipping profiles are something you may wish to set up before listing items, simply because it will make it easier for you when it comes time to list items for sale in your store. For more information on setting up shipping profiles, please see the chapter on shipping items.

Once you have taken some time to explore Etsy and the different items that have been posted for sale on the site and have gotten a good feel for the Etsy style, it should not take you long to create your profile and your store. As soon as you have set up your shop page, you can start listing your items for sale.

The First Sale

It's a great feeling to receive an e-mail from Etsy letting you know that you have sold an item from your shop, or, if you have the Etsy Seller app installed on your phone, to hear that "ka-ching" as a new sale comes in. But what do you do now?

You'll be able to find the details about your sale in the "Orders" section of your Etsy shop. It's a good idea to check to see if the buyer has included any special notes with the order. Sometimes a buyer will indicate a correction to his or her address, the explanation that this should be sent as a gift item, or some specific packing instructions.

You want to ship out orders as soon as you are able to do so. I generally ship out all orders the next business day. When you're ready to ship out the order, you can locate the details in the "Orders" section. If you like, print out a copy of the order or a gift receipt to include in the package as a packing slip.

Then it's time to pack up your order and either print a shipping label from Etsy or take it to your local post office to ship out. You can find more details about shipping out items in Chapter 5.

Getting Paid

Etsy buyers have the option of paying with a credit card directly through Etsy or using their PayPal account. Recently, Etsy also added an option that allows buyers to pay using Apple Pay or Google Wallet. For sellers, these mobile payments work similarly to credit card payments made via Etsy.

Etsy Direct Checkout enables shoppers to use their credit cards, PayPal, Etsy gift cards, Apple Pay, or Google Wallet to pay for their purchases. The funds are deposited directly into your Etsy account. They will be automatically disbursed to your bank account each Monday. (Note: when signing up for Etsy's Direct Checkout, you will need to include your bank account details.) Sellers also have the option to schedule earlier deposits if they want the money sooner. Deposits usually take a few days to appear in your bank account.

You may also opt to include your PayPal account, to collect payments directly from Etsy shoppers without using Etsy Direct Checkout. You can allow buyers the option of going through Etsy Direct Checkout to make a payment or paying you directly with PayPal. If you prefer not to receive payments to a PayPal account, shoppers can still use their PayPal accounts with Etsy Direct Checkout.

You can also use any money in your Etsy account to directly pay your Etsy bill. Your bill will include any listing fees and will also include any postage costs if you purchase your shipping labels through Etsy.

Reviews

Etsy uses a review system for buyers to provide feedback on sellers. There is no longer a feedback system for rating buyers. The review system allows shoppers to leave you up to five stars and a short note about their shopping experience. Obviously it's important to strive to please customers by accurately describing items, packing them carefully, and shipping them promptly. You want to make sure that most shoppers leave positive reviews with lots of stars.

Reviews are not quite as important as feedback is on other platforms such as eBay. While I've found that on sites such as eBay I receive feedback for almost every transaction, on Etsy I receive reviews on somewhere between a quarter and a third of my sales. Thankfully, these reviews are overwhelmingly positive.

When shoppers visit your shop or look at an item in your shop, they will see along the side panel a graphic representation of the average number of stars you've received, and when they click on these stars, they can see a list of the recent reviews. The star ranking and the reviews give reluctant shoppers the reassurance that you are a professional seller with a lot of pleased customers.

Chapter 2
Finding Inventory

Probably my favorite part of selling on Etsy is tracking down new inventory. It's like a treasure hunt. Though I don't mind prepping my items, taking photos, writing descriptions, and shipping my items, those steps feel a little bit more like work. Shopping, on the other hand, can be a lot of fun, and there are so many cool places to track down new old stuff to sell.

Thrift Stores

Thrift stores are probably the easiest way to get started sourcing Etsy inventory. They're open year round, and most are open enough hours that even if you have a day job or other commitments to attend to, you can still find some time to do some shopping during the store's operating hours.

If you're not familiar with the thrift stores in your area, the website TheThriftShopper.com offers a national directory of stores that you can search by zip code. This also comes in handy if you happen to be traveling or visiting someone out of town and want to do some inventory sourcing along the way. The site also has some user-written reviews of the different stores, which will give you an idea of what to expect at the store.

Thrift store chains such as Goodwill or the Salvation Army can be found all over and tend to be larger stores with pretty large inventories. Their policies and practices tend to be the same from store to store, so shoppers know what to expect, whether it's their hometown Sally or one in a neighboring area. While I visit these chain thrifts, I often do just as well, if not better, at some of the smaller thrift stores.

Most thrift stores raise funds for charities or nonprofit organizations of some sort, including churches, food pantries, animal shelters, and hospitals. So not only do you get to pick up some great deals, but you can feel good knowing that your money is going to be used to help others. Thrift stores receive their inventory as donations from individuals and sometimes retail stores. Thrift stores are staffed by a mixture of paid employees and volunteers, with the larger stores usually having a regular crew of paid staff and the smaller stores relying on volunteers.

Thrift store inventory and prices will vary from store to store and can vary from day to day. Part of the fun of visiting these secondhand shops is that you never know what you'll find. Some stores will separate out items that they deem vintage and place them in a special section of the shop, though even at these stores, I routinely find vintage items throughout the store. Most thrift stores don't segregate the vintage items and instead keep items grouped by category, such as kitchen stuff, stationery items, toys, and clothing.

After a few visits to different stores, you'll get a pretty good feel for the ones that have a decent number of vintage items and the ones that have the best prices on those vintage items. Of course, that doesn't mean you'll always find good stuff at these stores.

Tip: If a thrift store that you visit has an e-mail mailing list, sign up for it. This is a great way to learn about upcoming sales at the store or, in some cases, receive special discounts and coupons.

You'll want to familiarize yourself with the different sales and deals that the thrift stores in your area offer. For example, some stores, such as the Salvation Army, use colored tags to price their items, with a different color on sale each day. Sometimes this means all items with this color tag are on sale, but in other stores it might mean that only clothing is on sale. Certain stores will have a day when the whole store (or nearly the whole store) is on sale. This is generally every Wednesday at the Salvation Army, while other stores will sometimes have such sales once a month. Although lots of deals can be had on sale days, the stores tend to be extra crowded and you may have to contend with some competition and longer lines to check out.

Want to get a really good deal on items? Look for outlet thrift stores. The Goodwill runs outlets where goods are bought by the pound, and sometimes local thrift stores will have similar weigh-and-pay outlets. While you can pick up a lot of stuff extraordinarily cheap, such shops can be a bit intimidating. Veteran resellers warn new Goodwill weigh-and-pay shoppers to wear thick gloves when sorting through the bins of merchandise and to be prepared to deal with aggressive shoppers. It sounds a bit intimidating, but if you're the sort of shopper who likes a challenge, you might want to give it a try.

Rummage Sales

Outlet thrifts aren't the only place where you'll find aggressive shoppers. I've seen more than a few at rummage sales. The good news is that there are also a lot of very nice, well-behaved shoppers at such sales. A rummage sale is a sale that raises money for some sort of nonprofit organization. Many benefit churches, but I've also attended rummage sales that benefit volunteer fire departments, schools, and other organizations. Generally, a rummage sale is held over a period of a few days and may be held once or twice a year.

As with thrift stores, the policies and the wares at rummage sales can vary from sale to sale. Generally, all the usual stuff is there: household and kitchen stuff, games, books, and clothing. Most of the rummage sales I go to have extraordinarily cheap prices. I'm often able to purchase a large tote bag's worth of items for twenty dollars or less. In fact, some rummage sales will have fill-a-bag sales, usually on the last day of the sale, where they allow you to purchase everything you can fit into a bag for a set price, usually somewhere in the neighborhood of two to five dollars. If your funds for inventory are low, rummage sales can be a great way to score a lot of goods for only a little bit of money.

As the name suggests, rummage sales can be a bit of a mess. Most of the ones I've attended are in pretty cramped spaces, and since they usually have a lot of stuff for sale, that leads to things getting somewhat messy. That, coupled with the fact that there are often a lot of people in attendance, means that shopping can become a contact sport.

Rummage sales almost always have a set start time, say 9:00 a.m. Attendees will start to line up before then. Depending on how big and how popular the sale is, the line may start to form a half hour or more before the start of the sale. In seasonal places this might mean waiting outside in the rain or the cold, so dress appropriately and don't forget some nice, large (and sturdy!) tote bags to carry your treasures.

I find out about most of the rummage sales that I attend through advertisements in my local penny-saver newspaper. Many are also listed in the classifieds section of the local newspapers. Community bulletin boards and signs spotted along the side of the road have also led me to some rummage sales.

Garage Sales/Yard Sales

Just what they are called tends to depend as much on where you live as the type of structure they are held in, but whether you call it a garage sale, a yard sale, a tag sale, or a barn sale, it all pretty much amounts to the same thing: an individual or a family selling off stuff they no longer want or need. That means the type of goods and the prices can vary greatly. Because of this, and the fact that some may be located pretty far off the beaten track, garage/yard sales can be a risky proposition. That is, you might spend ten or fifteen minutes driving on twisting and turning back roads only to find there isn't anything you are interested in purchasing at the sale.

I find out about sales in my area through my local penny-saver newspaper. Free local weekly papers tend to be the best source for finding nearby garage sales. I prefer ads that use words such as "antique" or "vintage" or even simply "old stuff" because it makes me think I might actually find some stuff. What usually ends up happening is that I'll head out to track down a couple of sales I saw advertised in the paper, and, along the way, I'll see signs for a few more and stop there as well.

If you're planning on hitting garage sales, don't forget to bring lots of small bills with you. Prices do tend to be low, and there's no guarantee that the folks running the sale stocked up on change beforehand. If you enjoy haggling and making deals, the garage sale scene might be for you. Common etiquette at yard and garage sales is to price things a little high with the expectation that shoppers will offer less money. Some folks don't even bother to price their items and simply ask shoppers to make them an offer.

Estate Sales

An estate sale is sort of like a garage or yard sale, but at an estate sale, the whole contents of the house are usually up for sale. Many estate sales are run by professional estate-sale companies, though some are run by private individuals. More so than at a yard sale, prices on items at an estate sale tend to be clearly indicated.

One nice thing about an estate sale, especially those run by a professional company, is that you can often see some preview pictures of the sale ahead of time online. (The website EstateSales.net is a good resource for finding local estate sales.) This will give you an idea of the sorts of items that will be available at the sale, and it is usually a pretty good indication of whether or not it will be worth your time to attend.

Estate sales begin at a set time, and, like rummage sales, usually attract a crowd of shoppers who line up ahead of time. Estate sales prices tend to be a little bit higher than garage/yard sales prices, but you can still find some great deals. Haggling and cutting deals is part of the estate-sales game. With multiday sales, they will usually have a half-price day the last day of the sale.

Auctions

Auctions are another great resource for finding great deals on vintage treasures. I've managed to score huge amounts of inventory for very little money by shopping at auctions. Auctions will generally take more time than garage sales and estate sales, as they tend to be multihour events, but they also usually have a lot more goods than you'll find at your average estate sale or garage sale.

Auctions come in two varieties. The first type is those that are held at an auction house or a similar public building, such as a fire hall. The second type is those that are held on-site at a home, and these are often referred to as on-site estate auctions. In general, those that are held at auction halls have merchandise that has come from multiple estates, while on-site auctions usually have items from only one estate —but that doesn't mean these auctions have a shortage of stuff to buy. In fact, most of the on-site auctions I've attended have tons of stuff. In general, if folks are resorting to an auction to sell off items, that's usually because there's an overwhelming amount of stuff.

While you can usually find advertisements about upcoming local auctions in the classifieds section of your local newspaper, you can find more details and a full listing of upcoming sales at the website Auctionzip.com. Most of the auctions you will find there also include photos of a sampling of the items that will be available at the sale, which will give you a good idea of the type of things you'll find at the auction. Although this is usually only a small portion of the items that will be at the sale, you can usually tell whether or not the sale will include the sorts of thing that interest you.

Each auction company runs its sales differently, but in general most have a preview period before the auction begins, when prospective buyers can examine the items. So you'll want to show up early, if for no other reason than to get a look at what will be up for bid. You'll also want to show up early to find a parking spot, especially for on-site auctions; parking can get a bit crazy.

Finally, you'll need to allow yourself time to register to bid at the auction. Make sure to bring your driver's license or other state-issued photo ID, as most auction companies use these when registering you to bid. You'll receive your own lucky bidder number at this time. While auction houses usually provide their own seating, at an on-site auction you're on your own. If you aren't comfortable standing for two or more hours, bring a folding chair. Since on-site auctions are usually held outside, you'll want to dress appropriately—warm jackets in cooler weather and hats and sunblock during the warmer months.

If they don't tell you ahead of time in their advertisement or Auctionzip listing, auction companies will tell you on the day of the sale about when the different items will be auctioned. In general all the furniture will be auctioned at one time, smalls at another time, and box lots at another time. For especially large auctions, they may have two auctioneers going simultaneously to move stuff along.

Make sure to familiarize yourself with the auction terms before bidding so you know exactly how much you will be paying for any items you win. Is there a buyer's premium? Do they charge sales tax? What forms of payment are accepted? Note that many auctions that charge a buyer's premium will offer a discount to their premium for those bidders who pay in cash. In general, it's a good rule of thumb to bring lots of cash to an auction. I've yet to come across one that didn't accept cash as a form of payment!

Auctions can be a lot of fun and can be a great way to pick up a lot of inventory without breaking the bank. While some desirable items can get bid up very high, you'll be surprised at all the sellable items you can pick up for a song. I'm a big fan of box lots. Though some of these lots can get bid up high, many don't. Often, for one to five dollars, you can pick up items worth a hundred dollars or more when you sell them online.

The first auction I ever attended was an estate auction for someone who must have been something of a hoarder. There was an amazing amount of stuff at this auction, and, as the auctioneers reminded us a few times, all that stuff had come out of that little house. It was hard to believe. I only spent sixteen dollars, and my midsize SUV was packed to the gills with stuff. What's more, that sixteen-dollar investment led to hundreds of dollars' worth of Etsy sales. How did I get so much stuff for sixteen dollars? Box lots.

Most of the auctions I attend auction off box lots in groups, allowing winning bidders their choice of lots from the section. Auctioneers will go through a particular section until there are only a few box lots left and bidding has tapered off. At that point they'll offer the remaining lots as one lot—or for "one money," in auctionspeak—and that "one money" tends not to be more than a buck or two. This is why auctions are a great way to stock up on inventory, even when you don't have a big bankroll. It also means you can afford to take some chances on items you don't know too much about.

Here's an auction tip for you: stay until the end of the auction. Auctions run for a long time, and people start to get antsy or tired or need a bathroom break. That means that sometimes the last few things that come up for auction may not go for their full value. At one auction, one of the last items that came up was a lot that included an old camera and a case. I really had no idea what was in the lot, but I could see the camera case and figured that was worth at least a dollar. So, when no one was bidding, I offered a dollar, and for a buck wound up with three vintage cameras, several packages of new old stock film, an old portable reel-to-reel recorder, and an old voltmeter. That one-dollar bid ended up making me more than a hundred dollars after the different items had sold.

Now, one caveat about auctions, especially if you end up buying some big box lots, is that you will wind up with stuff that has no value to you. Sometimes I wonder if some of the pack rats and hoarders whose stuff has come up for auction got their start buying up box lots. In any case, you probably don't want all this junk cluttering up your house. Don't be afraid to throw out the stuff that has no value to you. Or, if you feel too bad about trashing stuff that someone maybe could use, donate it to a local thrift store or upcoming rummage sale.

The Seasonal Nature of Sourcing

It might seem that there are so many places to find vintage stuff to sell, you can't possibly run out of new old inventory. But, depending on where you live, sourcing tends to vary with the season. Those of us who live in four-season places are usually overwhelmed with inventory in the warmer months, but, come winter, things slow down and we might find our inventory dwindling. In the colder months, thrift stores, auction-house auctions, and the occasional estate sale tend to be the only sources of new stock, and all of these places tend to be a little more crowded since all local resellers are in the same boat.

Cold-weather Etsy sellers may want to follow the example of squirrels and stockpile some of their summer treasures for the winter months. Or perhaps you'd rather mimic the behavior of birds and head south for a week or two during the winter, where you can still find lots of new inventory and won't have to worry about shoveling any snow.

Chapter 3
What to Sell

Etsy allows the sale of items twenty years old or older in the vintage category, but that's a pretty broad range of items. What sort of items you choose to sell will depend on what you are most interested in, what you are able to locate, or simply what you think would be easiest to ship and store. You have the option of carrying a broad range of items in your Etsy store or specializing in a certain type or style of product.

How Do You Know if It's Vintage?

One question new vintage sellers might have is how to determine how old an item is. Twenty years isn't all that long ago, especially to those of us who are still coming to terms with the fact that the clothing we wore in high school is now technically vintage. There are a lot of clues to help determine how old an item is. Some items, such as books, games, and other printed materials will often have a date right on them, meaning you don't have to do any guesswork. Other items, such as china and ceramic items, are often stamped at the bottom or have a sticker indicating where they were manufactured. For example, most of these items that are marked Made in Japan are probably vintage, since these days very little is made in Japan. On the other hand, if another Asian country, namely China, is listed as the place of manufacture, there's a good chance that it's not all that old. The materials used, the style, and the overall condition will provide clues as to how old something is. The good news is that the more you've been doing this, the easier it will be for you to recognize a vintage item versus a newer item at a glance. Of course, for those cases when you need more than a glance, such as when you need to read tiny printing on the bottom or backside of an object, it might be helpful to keep a pair of reading glasses or a magnifying glass handy, especially if, like me, you're in the camp where your high school clothes are now vintage.

Here is a by-no-means-exhaustive list of some vintage items you can sell on Etsy:

Old Technology

For sellers who are interested in finding some higher-value items, outdated technology offers a lot of possibilities. There are some challenges when it comes to listing these items, though. The biggest issue is determining whether or not an item is still in working condition. While you can always sell items in as-is, untested condition, you'll be able to command a higher price if you can confirm that an item actually works. Another issue you'll run into with a lot of (though by no means all) old tech stuff is shipping. A lot of this stuff tends to be big, bulky, and heavy. If you're not yet comfortable with estimating shipping costs, you might want to pass up the heavier, bulkier items for now so that you don't get burned on the shipping charges.

There's a wide variety of old technology that can be sold on Etsy. Here are some items that sell pretty reliably:

Typewriters

Being a writer, I'm kind of partial to old typewriters. Of course, I would never consider trying to write a book on one. Typewriters simply can't match the ease and convenience of writing a book on a laptop, but they sure do look pretty.

Typewriters tend to be long-tail items. They will sell, but in my experience they take some time to sell. This can be a problem if you're short on storage space because typewriters, even what they used to call "portable" ones, can take up a lot of room. On the plus side, typewriters usually sell for a decent chunk of change. They start at about $40 to $50 and, depending on the make and model, can go as high as $300 or more. What's especially cool about typewriters is that you can often pick them up relatively inexpensively. I've bought typewriters for three dollars or less, and I've picked up at least three awesome old typewriters for a grand total of zero dollars.

To completely test a typewriter, you'll want to have a ribbon in the machine. Most of the typewriters I've come across over the years still have their old ribbons installed, and if you advance the ribbon on the spool, there's usually enough ink on the ribbon to give at least a faint impression on a piece of paper.

Even if you don't have a decent ribbon in the machine, you can test the mechanics of the device. Do the keys type without sticking? Does the carriage return work? (Note: Many typewriters have a carriage lock to prevent the carriage from sliding when porting the machine around. Don't mistake your typewriter for being broken when all you need to do is unlock it.) Does the roller spin freely?

When determining whether or not to buy an old typewriter, there are some factors to consider. Manual typewriters (as opposed to electric typewriters) are the best bet. Looks matter a great deal when it comes to typewriters, since very few customers are buying them for anything other than display purposes. When hunting for typewriters, look for great vintage styling and distinctive colors. Some brands that are reliable sellers are Olivetti, Olympia, Royal, and Underwood.

Typewriters can be challenging to ship. They're often very heavy and generally don't fit into any sort of flat-rate packaging. Weighing a typewriter along with the box you intend to ship it in before you list it may be a good idea so you can see about how much it will cost to ship to different areas.

Cameras

Cameras are another bit of old tech that tends to sell well on Etsy. In most cases, they are relatively easy to ship, certainly a lot easier and less expensive than typewriters. The drawback with cameras is that unless you are someone with a passion for film photography, testing your vintage camera may not be feasible. The good news is that you can still make money selling vintage cameras on Etsy. I certainly have.

While there can be a lot of money to be made in expensive, high-end cameras, I leave that to the photography types. Folks buying cameras on Etsy, though, aren't always looking for a camera they can use for taking pictures. Many buyers are looking for something to display on a shelf, add to a collection, or use as a prop, and untested cameras work just fine for those purposes.

In this case, what you want to look for is great vintage styling. Any camera with a distinct old-school look will likely appeal to shoppers looking for display cameras. Of special interest are the cameras that stand out from the pack—something in a color other than the standard black or something iconic, such as the beige Polaroid with the rainbow stripe decal (I've personally sold a couple of those). The value of a vintage camera will depend on its rarity and overall condition—in the case of an untested camera, its physical appearance—but on average, a nice-looking vintage camera that may or may not work can fetch twenty to forty dollars, perhaps more if it's especially unusual. Don't think that cameras have to be high quality to be valuable. Even a very cheaply made plastic camera that looks very vintage can bring in twenty to twenty-five dollars.

Camera accessories can also be valuable. Camera bags, flash bulbs, old film canisters, and old rolls of film all sell well on Etsy. Such products sell well to collectors as well as photographers.

I'm going to close this section on cameras with a story of a great camera haul. It was almost the end of a long, hot estate auction, and a box of miscellaneous camera stuff came up to the auction block. Some folks had already started to pack up their stuff and settle up with the cashier. The bidding started at ten dollars, dropped to five, and then to one. I didn't even know what it was, but I figured that the camera bag I could see had to be worth at least a dollar, so I raised my auction number in the air and was the winner and sole bidder of a one-dollar lot of assorted stuff. It wasn't until we got everything home that we decided to go through it. There were three old cameras, the camera bag, an old portable reel-to-reel recorder, an old voltameter, and some miscellaneous camera accessories including several rolls of film. It was definitely worth well more than the dollar I had spent on it.

But as I was sorting out the stuff from that box, I almost made a big mistake. I almost discarded the rolls of film. There were seven rolls altogether in two different formats. One roll was loose; the others were all sealed in their original boxes with expiration dates that were decades past. I set the film aside thinking maybe somebody might have interest in it for some sort of display. When I researched it, I realized that old, expired film is not worthless. I grouped the film into two lots. One lot had four rolls of film, two of which were Kodak.

The other two were a no-name brand. That lot sold for twenty dollars. The lot with the three sealed Kodak rolls and one loose roll sold for twenty-five. Glad I didn't rashly decide to chuck that old film in the trash!

Phones

I've sold a number of old rotary phones on Etsy over the years. Old phones can be heavy but oftentimes will fit into a flat-rate shipping box, so they aren't too much of a chore to ship. Testing them will require an active landline. Don't have one? Make friends with someone who does. At least that's my strategy!

Any rotary phone has value. Like so much old technology, even if it's in nonworking condition, it has value as a prop or a display piece. If you can test a phone and prove that it's in working order, you will be able to get a little bit more for it than a nonworking or untested phone.

The value of old phones can vary widely. At the low end, a non-functioning or untested phone in a more common style may be worth only twenty dollars. But phones in a more distinctive or rare style will command higher prices. Tan and black are probably the most common colors for old rotary phones. So red, yellow, or other colored phones will be worth more. If the phone is something other than the standard boxy desk phone, this too will increase the value. If it's something especially rare and funky looking, the phone could be worth hundreds of dollars.

Even the more modern push-button phones can have value if they have a fun or different sort of style or come in an unusual color. I suppose if you wait long enough, even your cell phone will have value as a vintage collectible.

Record Players, Radios, and Tape Players

I've always done well with vintage music technology. These pieces tend to hold a lot of nostalgia value for people, but most folks are looking for a working device, so testing is important.

I've only ever been lucky enough to come across a couple of vintage portable record players, but I ended up selling both for a nice profit. On Etsy, the less expensive, portable-style players usually have more value than a higher-end turntable. The good news is that these devices are a little easier to ship, and, since they generally have built-in speakers, they are easier to test. Distinctive or kitschy styles tend to offer the greatest return, but any vintage portable record player has value. You should be able to sell a portable player in working condition for anywhere from $30 to $85, depending on style and condition. A few especially rare players can be worth upward of $200. You'll need a record to test out a record player. The good news is that these can usually be picked up inexpensively at thrift stores, garage sales, or rummage sales. If it's been a few years since you've used a record player, don't forget, when testing, to make sure the record player is set for the appropriate speed. Often 45-RPM records will require a plastic adapter to be used with the hole in the center. Some players come with an adapter.

Radios are one of those items that can vary widely in price on Etsy. On the low end, vintage radios sell for $20, and on the high end, you're looking at $500 or more. There are a lot of factors that determine a radio's value. Obviously the more distinctive the style, the more money the radio will be worth. Old radios with a body made out of actual wood tend to be pretty valuable, but there are plenty of plastic-bodied radios that can still bring in some big bucks. Condition also plays a big role in a radio's value. Aesthetically, it should look nice, but more importantly, it should work. The good news is that most radios are easy to test. In most cases, all you'll need is an electrical outlet or, in the case of battery-operated radios, some batteries that you know are not dead. If your radio is working, you'll hear some static once you turn it on, and then, as you turn the dial, you'll hear a station or two. Radios come in all shapes and sizes. Some, such as transistor radios and smaller portable radios, can be shipped easily in smaller boxes or, depending on the item weight, in some flat-rate boxes. The larger radios, which also tend to be the more valuable ones, will present some shipping challenges due to their weight and often-bulky sizes.

I've only ever sold a few tape players on Etsy, but that's because I've only been lucky enough to find a few. As with any other sort of old technology, functionality and styling will determine the tape player's value. Because of their nostalgia value, even cheap tape players that were designed for use by children can be valuable on Etsy, especially if they are still in working condition. Like record players, you'll need a tape to test out your tape player, and probably batteries too, if it's a portable one.

Other Gadgets

Just about any old technology has value on Etsy, but functionality will go a long way toward determining that value. That's why some nonelectronic tech is usually a good bet. Slide rules are a reliable seller, and while they can become broken or cracked, this tends to be rare. Things were made better back in the day, and all the slide rules I've come across have survived intact. In general they're worth ten to twenty dollars or perhaps more, depending on the brand and condition. But since you can often pick them up for a dollar and they are easy to ship and store, they provide a nice return on investment.

Various old gizmos and tools have a special appeal for many male shoppers on Etsy. What the item does; whether or not it works; and if it comes with all its components, an instruction manual, and, best of all, an original box can really make a huge difference in the price someone is willing to pay for an item. A lot of these will be long-tail items that might take longer to sell, waiting for the collector looking for that unusual or hard-to-find gadget.

Nostalgic items are always very successful on Etsy, and anything that reminds a shopper of something he or she had as a kid will usually fetch big bucks. Old technology that was geared toward children or was a toy or game of any sort tends to be a little bit more difficult to find in good condition, but if you can locate some and the price is right, snatch it up. Things like kids' clocks, handheld video games, and toy radios all can sell for a lot of money on Etsy.

Toys

Toys in general do very well on Etsy thanks to the nostalgia market, and while the prices may not be quite as high as they are for some other items, they're reliable and relatively quick sellers. Here are some toys to be on the lookout for:

Plush

I love old stuffed animals because I've done really well selling them on Etsy. They have a couple of things going for them. First of all, they are usually inexpensive; rarely do they cost more than a dollar. Second, they are nice and easy to ship—no need to worry about them breaking in transit.

I like older stuffed animals, which can usually be identified by both their style and any tags that may be attached to them. I've sold vintage teddy bears and other stuffed animals for forty dollars—not bad for a one-dollar or less investment. Beyond age and distinctive styling, other things that can contribute to stuffed animals' value might be unique colors or designs or licensed characters that can be firmly identified as a particular decade. These will have appeal to those looking to replace something they owned as a child. And an animal with unique colors or designs will be easier for an Internet searcher to track down.

Something that's been a reliable seller for me, if not a high-value item, are stuffed animals and small shaped pillows made from cut-and-sew printed fabric panels. These are flat, two-dimensional-style stuffies that were likely made at home, and they can feature licensed designs as well as general shapes and creatures.

When shopping for plush, there are some things to consider. One thing you want to note is an item's condition. Is it especially dirty? Perhaps more importantly, what does it smell like? Does it have a musty odor? Does it smell like cigarettes? I would suggest leaving behind these problem items, as they probably won't sell, and who wants to get stuck with some stinky, dirty thing? One thing to keep in mind is that some thrift stores have made the decision to no longer carry stuffed animals due to the risk of bed-bug contamination. If you live in or near an area that has experienced bed-bug infestations, you might want to skip the stuffed animals, though for the most part I would say these items are probably safe.

Dollhouse Miniatures

One of my favorite toy items to sell is dollhouse furniture and other miniatures. These are not high-value items. I think the most I've ever sold a dollhouse piece for is twenty dollars, but, like stuffed animals, dollhouse furniture and accessories can often be found at very inexpensive prices. Oftentimes you will find a lot or set of it grouped together at a sale or store.

This is something that tends to do better on Etsy when you break up the lot and sell each piece or a set of coordinating pieces individually. I've found that dollhouse furnishings move pretty quickly, and they are one of those items whose size makes them easy to store and easy to ship.

Dolls

Dolls have a pretty dedicated and devoted group of collectors, and for this reason it may be a bit tough for someone inexperienced to start selling dolls. Many auctions I've gone to that had dolls also had a corresponding number of doll collectors in attendance. But there are times when you might stumble upon a collectible doll for a price you can't pass up.

With things such as mint, in-package dolls, you might be best off selling them via an eBay auction, but for dolls that still have a nice vintage style but might not be quite as collectible, Etsy may be a better fit for them. Condition can play a big part in a doll's value. So check to make sure the joints are in good condition and that there is no damage to the doll.

Kitschy dolls or those that can be placed in a specific time period or decade, such as Holly Hobbie and other ragamuffin-style dolls from the late 1970s to early 1980s, will sell well on Etsy. Prices can vary wildly for dolls, but even those that might not be as popular with serious doll collectors can still have value to those hoping to replace a treasured toy from their childhood.

Don't forget about less conventional dolls, such as paper dolls. Their flimsy nature means a lot fewer of them have made it through the years intact. They'll be the most valuable in uncut condition, though even cut-out ones with their original box or packaging will hold some value. The most valuable will be those based on celebrities or television or movie characters.

Games

Games are something I come across pretty often in my travels, and I've done quite well on some of the vintage ones. For the most part, games are a quick-selling item. One thing to keep in mind with games is that some, due to their size and weight, can be expensive to ship, so you'll need to factor that in when considering their value. That said, some of the heaviest games out there, backgammon sets, are very reliable sellers for me, and full-size sets priced at forty dollars with roughly a seventeen-dollar shipping price usually sell within a month of my listing them on Etsy.

If you hate the idea of storing and shipping big heavy things, look for smaller games. Playing cards are something that's nice and easy to store and ship, and they sell regularly on Etsy. A nice deck of vintage cards with a fun illustration on the backs will fetch between six and ten dollars, depending on condition. Single decks can be shipped via First Class Mail. You can usually find vintage decks of cards for a dollar or less.

With playing cards and any game, missing pieces can greatly decrease the value of your item. It's important to check through and make sure everything is there. With classic or standard games such as playing cards or chess and backgammon sets, this is easy enough to do, but with more unusual vintage games, which can be worth some money, this may be more difficult. Included instruction manuals might give you the answers you need, or you might try to see if anyone on a forum or site online has catalogued what all the pieces are for a given game. Either way, it's a good idea to be clear in your description about what and how many of each piece is included with the game.

Even when a game or deck of cards is incomplete, it can still have value. Mismatched playing cards and other ephemera items can be lotted together and sold on Etsy to crafters and scrapbookers. The same is true of game pieces and tiles, though single game pieces or cards can be sold and purchased (I've done the latter when I had games with missing parts) on eBay.

Puzzles

Speaking of something where having all the pieces can make a huge difference, vintage jigsaw puzzles are another item that can do well on Etsy in the right condition. Of course, unless you are a big fan of doing puzzles, you might want to avoid large puzzles that aren't in sealed packages, because the only way to test to make sure the set is complete is to actually put it together. That's why if I'm selling a puzzle on Etsy, it's either new old stock—that is, still sealed up and never used—or it's one of those mini puzzles, which have the added advantage of being easy to ship and store.

Miscellaneous Toys

When I'm out sourcing, I'm drawn to toys of all sorts. I guess that's the kid in me. I like toys because they are colorful, and many have such iconic styling. I guess I also like them because I've done well selling them. Some of the toys I've sold over the years include old View-Masters, vintage Fisher-Price toys, assorted old wooden toys, toy soldiers and other sets, toy tea sets, and vintage wooden blocks.

Condition and style can play a big part in determining an item's value. New old-stock items, even of relatively cheap toys, can be a good investment. Toys that might have been licensed to accompany the release of a movie or a television show will have some interest for collectors as well as those reliving childhood memories. The values for old toys are all over the map and will depend on an item's condition and rarity.

Clothing and Accessories

There is a huge market on Etsy for vintage wearable items, whether it's a dress or something smaller such as a scarf or a necktie. There are some vintage Etsy shops that deal exclusively in vintage clothing, and you would be surprised how much money some old clothes can fetch.

You'll often find vintage garments at thrift stores and rummage sales, though be warned that in most cases this means sorting through all the clothes to find a few vintage treasures. For some this task might seem overwhelming, but others might love this sort of challenge.

Some of the least challenging vintage clothing items to deal with can bring in some pretty nice money. Vintage T-shirts have a big collectors' market. Part of the problem is that a lot of these shirts were worn until they fell apart and ended their lives by becoming dust rags, but those that have miraculously survived through the years can be resold for good money even in worn condition. Some things to be on the lookout for with vintage T-shirts include comic book and cartoon characters, old TV shows, concert T-shirts, and anything that has a distinctly vintage illustration or saying. Another easy-to-deal-with item is vintage baseball caps. Value will vary depending on the condition, theme, and rarity, but the more retro it looks, the more likely you'll be able to make a nice profit on it.

Things such vintage handkerchiefs and scarves are very easy to deal with. Hankies do better when they have a really unique print or illustration. Look for hankies that are signed by a particular designer. Scarves are another item where the more unique and interesting a design is, the better it will do. I've had particularly good success with souvenir scarves and the handful of souvenir hankies that I've been lucky enough to come across.

Vintage hats and gloves are something that I routinely come across in my travels. Things such as dress gloves and ladies' dress hats used to be all the rage but have fallen out of fashion in recent times, making vintage ones special to those hoping to create a vintage look. Some vintage hats were crafted of such delicate materials that they've only just barely survived. That said, even vintage hats with things such as torn netting can still find eager buyers on Etsy, where shoppers don't mind taking steps to fix up and resurrect older pieces. Something I've noticed with all clothing, but especially with gloves, is that women were definitely smaller way back when. Most of the gloves I find are of supersmall sizes that won't fit the hands of most modern women. Gloves do have standard sizes, though you might not find tags inside all the vintage gloves you come across. Be sure to note the size or approximate size in your listing and give measurements so that buyers can determine whether or not a glove will fit them.

Vintage eyewear is something that does very well on Etsy, and it can command a high selling price. This includes both vintage prescription glasses as well as vintage sunglasses, both prescription and non. The nice thing about vintage glasses is that I'm forever finding them at thrift stores and rummage sales for very affordable prices. With nonprescription sunglasses, what buyers are looking for is something they can wear as is, while with prescription glasses, what you're really selling is the frame so that the buyer most likely can replace the lenses with the prescription or nonprescription lenses of his or her choice. With a lot of modern items made to look old, it can be difficult to tell modern stuff from old stuff, but there are some clues. Country of manufacture can be a clue. If it was made in China, it's probably not vintage. American-made and European-made glasses are not guaranteed to be vintage, but they have a better shot. Look at brand names, and also look at the plastic or metal used. Though it's not a hard-and-fast rule, a lot of vintage plastic tends to be of a thicker, higher grade, and it often has a less shiny texture than modern stuff.

Always take the time to examine items carefully, and if you're anything like me, you'll want to remember to bring a pair of reading glasses with you so that you can make out the tiny printing that appears on the temples of glasses. I was in a thrift store one day and thought I'd discovered an awesome score. There in the locked case where they kept the more expensive items was a glasses case that said Carolina Herrera with a pair of vintage-looking ladies' sunglasses inside it. A decent pair of vintage Carolina Herrera sunglasses can fetch over a hundred dollars on Etsy, and these were priced at fifteen dollars. I asked to take a closer look at the sunglasses, already imagining the big money I was going to make on them, only to see on closer inspection that the sunglasses were a very cheap pair that had been placed inside the Carolina

Herrera case. Bummer, but at least I didn't make a fifteen-dollar mistake.

When it comes to clothing, look for distinctive styling, high quality, and good condition. Although you can still sell flawed items, they will sell for less money. It's a good idea to wash vintage garments before selling them, but because of the delicate nature of these older garments, you want to wash on a delicate cycle, or, better yet, by hand.

With clothing, one thing you'll want to consider is the best ways to photograph the garments for listing. You usually have two options. The first is to use a model. It doesn't necessarily need to be a professional model if you have a friend or relative who might be up for the task, but the model, as per Etsy's terms, will need to sign a release. Your other option—and this may be less of a hassle—is to use a mannequin or dress form of some sort. Although you can also photograph garments simply hung on a hanger or lay them flat on a table, this usually won't give shoppers a very clear idea of what the article actually looks like when worn.

With clothing, keep in mind that vintage sizes and modern sizes are two very different beasts. Always provide accurate measurements of things such as bust/chest, waist, hips, inseam, and length so that shoppers can determine whether or not an item will fit them or not.

Not sure about getting into the clothing market? Most accessory items are much easier to deal with than clothes, and while they are usually worth less, you can still make good money with them. I've done well with accessory items such as handkerchiefs, scarves, ties, and wallets. Condition and style will have a big impact on how much an item is worth and how quickly it will sell.

Jewelry

Like dolls, jewelry is one of those areas that seem to have a large and devoted following. There is big money to be made in vintage costume jewelry, but there's also a lot of competition for those items at auctions and other sales. One nice thing about jewelry is that it is perfect for online sellers since it is so easy to ship and pretty easy to store. I'll be honest: most of the jewelry I've sold has been stuff that I inherited as opposed to stuff I actually purchased.

I've probably sold as many jewelry boxes as I've sold articles of jewelry. Because of this, jewelry boxes are something I seek out. Sometimes, especially at an auction, jewelry boxes are sold already filled with jewelry. This could be a good way to get into the jewelry market, though you may find yourself in a bidding war with the serious jewelry buyers, who always seem to be at auctions.

One reason that there's so much interest in jewelry at sales is that valuable jewelry that contains precious stones or metals often gets mixed up with the less valuable costume stuff. Those hunting for gold and other valuable items usually come with their own jeweler's loupes and examine items carefully. Because of this, if you do wind up with some jewelry to list, make sure to look it over carefully before you do so. You don't need a loupe, but a magnifying glass might be useful. Look for markings on clasps and the underside of pieces to make sure what you're selling really is a costume piece and not something far more valuable.

Stationery and Paper Items

Something that's a reliable seller for me, if not a huge moneymaker, is stationery sets. I love vintage writing paper, and, apparently, I'm not alone. Rummage sales and thrift stores have been a pretty reliable source of vintage stationery sets, and these can go for anywhere from eight to twenty dollars on Etsy, depending on condition, quantity, and design. A set with its original box is worth more than loose sheets and envelopes, but all will sell well, especially if the set features distinctive vintage styling.

Vintage greeting cards are another reliable seller on Etsy. This is something that does better in a set than individually due to shipping costs. If you're lucky enough to stumble upon a bunch of cards that go together (it does happen from time to time; trust me!), you can list them as a set. Otherwise, what I try to do is set aside cards that I find until I have enough to warrant a listing. I would say a minimum of six is probably best. You can group cards by occasion or make your own mixed lot of vintage greeting cards.

I've also done well with vintage invitation sets. Some of them are still in sealed packets; others are partly used. Again, the more you have, the better, since someone likely wants to invite more than, say, three people to his or her next event.

While in general you want unused stationery items, there are exceptions. One notable one is postcards, which have value in both unused and used condition. Postcards can vary widely depending on their subject matter, age, and condition, and, like many other items, they have a very devoted audience of collectors. Even those that don't appeal to collectors might have interest for those looking to put together displays or even decorate their homes with some images of their local area from times gone by.

Photographs are another vintage item that can be desirable. The more unusual they are, the more money they will fetch. You'll also do better with photographs that have some identifying information on them. One day when going through some old photos at my grandmother's house, we found an old black-and-white snapshot of two young boys beside some towering plants. We wondered who they were and found the less-than-helpful identification "measuring the gilia." So don't be surprised if most of the vintage photos you come across have nothing useful written on the back. Even photos of random strangers can do well online for people who collect such items or who just want some old pictures to decorate their space. The oldest photographs will be printed on metal, and these will usually be worth a little more than paper photos. That said, the tintypes and old daguerreotypes are almost all portrait photos or perhaps landscapes, since the nature of old-fashioned photography required a longer time for the camera to capture the image. This is also why you seldom see folks smiling in really old photos—it's too hard to hold a smile for that long without it looking like a grimace. I've purchased old photos at an assortment of places, including auctions, rummage sales, book sales, and garage sales. Sometimes you'll end up with a whole album of photos, and usually the best course of action is to remove the photos and sell them individually or perhaps in thematically linked sets.

Maps are another paper item that I've had a lot of success with. While old road maps usually aren't that exciting, vintage maps that are more decorative in nature or that were issued for different recreational purposes have been big sellers for me. At the low end, such maps have sold for twenty dollars and at the high end fifty. That's nice because usually these can be picked up inexpensively. Over the years, I've picked up a number of maps at book sales. Even though they aren't actually books, they often get lumped in with them, and they can often be picked up for one to two dollars. Most maps fold up nicely for storage and mailing. Some roll up and will need to be shipped in a mailing tube. Those buying maps are usually using them to decorate their spaces and are interested in old but distinctive-looking maps that show the town or region they live in. For this reason, regional maps are probably a quicker sell than maps that cover a larger area such as, say, a whole country or the whole world.

Similar in some ways to maps are posters. They too are used to decorate walls, and they come in both fold-up and roll-up styles. I'll be honest: some posters that I thought were awesome sat unsold in my shop for years, while others sold quickly and for decent money. Again, posters can vary widely in price, but most of the ones I've sold have gone for forty dollars and up. The posters that I had the most success with were educational in nature, designed for use in classrooms. These posters are usually colorful, and the older ones have great vintage illustrations. Many of the old school posters are of the fold-up variety, making them nice and easy to ship. I've picked up posters at book sales as well as rummage and yard sales.

Speaking of old school posters, if you're lucky enough to come across an old pull-down classroom map or poster, you'll want to consider investing in it. Yes, this is one of those items that are a bit more challenging to ship, but they are reliable Etsy sellers and will bring in a hundred dollars or more, depending on condition and subject matter.

Books

Since I'm an author, it probably comes as no surprise that I'm something of a bibliophile. So I'm always a sucker for buying a cool or interesting book, and, as the overcrowded bookshelves in my house can attest, I do keep a fair number of the books I buy. But some of them I go ahead and sell online.

For the most part, single books don't do that well unless one is exceptional. The older a book is, the more likely selling it as an individual item will work —a family Bible from the 1800s, say, or maybe something like a yearbook or an older souvenir-style book, will do well as an individual item. There are other selling venues that specialize in books, and you might have better luck selling books through those sites.

Book sets and book lots, on the other hand, can do very well on Etsy. If you have some books that are all volumes from the same series, then it's a no-brainer to group them together and sell them as a set. From my experiences, these sets do very nicely on Etsy. But you can also sell sets of books that aren't part of the same series, and there are some different ways to go about putting your own book sets together.

One angle to go with is the decorative approach. Keep in mind that Etsy attracts those interested in interior design and those who are very visual. What these folks are looking for in terms of book sets may have nothing to do with the content of the books. I've sold sets of six or more hardcover books that were all the same or varying shades of the same color. I've also sold sets of books that were in the colors of the rainbow. The only thing to keep in mind with decorator lots is that the books should be in decent condition, or, if worn, it should be the sort of wear that gives the book character and not the sort that looks ugly. In most cases, decorator sets are sold without dust jackets, and it's the cloth covers in a particular shade or a range of shades that buyers are interested in. Make sure at least one photo shows the spines as the books would look on a bookshelf, since this is likely what the buyer is most interested in.

Another approach to consider with book lots is to look for a set that is thematically linked in some way. The theme can be as vague or as specific as you choose. Perhaps you find yourself with several vintage books about horses. A horse book set might appeal to someone who has a passion for horses or maybe is looking for some books to decorate a horse-themed room. Broader topics such as animals or even children's novels could also work. I've done well selling sets of literary classics. Who doesn't want to appear well read by displaying some classic literature on his or her shelf? And all the better if those classic books are distinctive-looking older editions.

Books are inventory you can find at a variety of places. The usual haunts, such as thrift stores, auctions, and yard sales, often offer a ready supply of books, but there are also used book sales devoted exclusively to the sale of books. Many of these are held as fundraisers by libraries. Some will have bag sale days where you can pick up an entire bag of books for five dollars, a great way to build up some sets to sell on Etsy.

Books can be quite heavy and expensive to ship, but in the United States, you always have the option to ship books via Media Mail at a substantial discount. Of course, you get what you pay for. Media Mail is notoriously slow. For this reason, I do not set it as my default shipping method on Etsy for book sets but do invite interested shoppers to contact me for the Media Mail rate if they don't need their books in a hurry.

Housewares and Kitchenwares

Decorators like to adorn their spaces with more than just pretty books, so items for the home or kitchen are a natural fit for Etsy. While some styles, in particular Midcentury Modern, are hugely popular, anything that has a fun or funky vintage style can do well on Etsy. Any size item can be sold on Etsy, including pieces of furniture, but new sellers will probably want to stick with something a little bit easier to ship. Vases, candlesticks, and bookends are all things that I've sold often on Etsy, and they usually aren't too much of a chore to ship. I've also sold things such as magazine holders and lamps, but that starts getting into difficult-to-ship territory.

Paintings and other wall hangings can be hit or miss in terms of shipping. Whether or not an item is in a frame and how big that frame is can have a big impact on how easy it is to box up and ship out. Of course, you can always liberate a bulky item from its frame, especially if the frame isn't anything too spectacular, and you can easily dispose of the frame.

Small wall shelves or knickknack shelves tend to be popular Etsy items, and if they aren't too large, they can fit nicely into a Priority Mail box. But the bigger they are, the more of a pain they will be to ship. It's also a good idea to think about where you will be storing items until they sell. This isn't such a problem with smaller items, but the larger the item, the more quickly you will find yourself running out of storage space.

Retro kitchen stuff has a huge market on Etsy, and the good news is that a lot of this stuff is small enough to easily ship, whether it's adorable salt and pepper shakers, desirable matching canister sets, or trivets with sassy sayings. Shipping shouldn't be too much of a headache, and you'll find a ready supply of inventory at thrift stores, rummage sales, and garage sales.

Rarer items such as Pyrex mixing-bowl sets or complete sets of vintage drinking glasses can be more of a challenge to ship. But they can be worth quite a bit of money depending on the pattern and the condition, so you might want to take a chance on such items. As always, style will be a huge factor in how quickly and for how much money your item sells.

Office and School Supplies

I love vintage office stuff, and that just might have something to do with the fact that I've done so well selling it on Etsy. I've found that office items are not as easy to come by as things such as collectibles or housewares, but usually what I do find moves quickly on Etsy.

Office items can roughly be divided into two categories: items that were designed for home offices and items that were designed for professional offices. Despite its original purpose, almost all of it now will be used in the home office.

Those items that were designed for home office use tend to look more decorative and fancy. While most of the modern home-office stuff is kind of bland and unappealing, vintage stuff tended to be a lot flashier, whether it was a leather or printed metal mail sorter, an ornate wooden file box, or maybe a nice marble pen holder. All are items that will do well on Etsy. Though strictly speaking they are not exclusive to office use, vintage globes tend to be popular on Etsy, and they add a nice vintage touch to the modern home office.

Those items that were designed for the working world have a completely different look and tend to be more utilitarian in nature, but don't think this makes them less desirable. This is exactly the style that some shoppers are looking for. Make sure to select "Industrial" from Etsy's list of styles on the listing page and also use the word in your title, description, and tags. Old company office accessories include things such as staplers, metal organizers, and signage.

For those who have the room to store and don't mind shipping large items, things such as metal cubbies, old office chairs, and vintage fans can be worth quite a bit of money. The high price tag and high shipping costs might mean these items don't move quite as quickly as other items, but the nice profit margin can make up for these issues.

Though technically not an "office" product, old school supplies, particularly old classroom and teacher items, can be very valuable on Etsy. I've already mentioned old classroom posters, but other educational products, including kits, models, other classroom decor, and motivational rubber stamps, have a lot of appeal to collectors, those trying to relive their childhood years, or anyone hoping to add a bit of vintage schoolroom to his or her decor. Part of the reason such items have held their value is that a lot have not survived the years. Items were worn out by students or discarded by schools and teachers. So you'll likely not find a lot of old classroom stuff when you're out searching, but if you do locate some stuff, snatch it up.

Vintage school supplies of all sorts, including pencil boxes, lunch boxes, and even things such as pencils and erasers, will find ready buyers on Etsy. Some items such as lunch boxes and erasers, particularly those in fun colors and shapes, have a big collector's market and can make you a decent amount of money. In the collectible eraser market, one brand to be on the lookout for is Diener. They made figural rubber erasers in the shapes of animals, vehicles, and cartoon characters. The solid-colored erasers are always stamped Diener, and some can be very valuable. These do nicely when sold in lots—unless, of course, one is a very rare Diener that can be sold for a high price on its own.

Collectibles

Collectibles is a pretty broad category and includes things that were specifically issued as collectible items, such as figurines and toys, as well as a host of other items that have become collectible over the years. Really, just about any vintage item that you sell on Etsy is probably a collectible to someone. Many, though, have no other purpose other than to add to a collection. This includes:

License Plates

License plates are not super valuable on Etsy, but since you can usually find old ones at rummages sales and yard sales for a buck or two, you can easily make a profit on them. I regularly sell old license plates for eight dollars, but for more if they are older or more rare. If it's listed anywhere on the tag, be sure to include the date. In some cases, a license plate buyer is looking to decorate a garage or room with vintage license plates or maybe even complete a collection of plates from all fifty states. But some buyers may want to use a plate with a restored car when they show it at car shows, in which case the date is key. Seldom will you find a license plate in clean condition, and if you do, you might want to investigate to make sure it's a genuine vintage item. After all, most license plates were used on cars and were subject to the weather and perils of the road. Dings and rust marks just add to the charm of a vintage license plate.

Old Advertising

Another type of collectible that often finds its way into decorating, particularly the man-cave style of decorating, is old advertising pieces. Such items are much sought after and can be very valuable, but for this reason they also can be priced expensively when you are out hunting for them. That said, you might still stumble upon a deal or two. Depending on how large a piece is, you will want to keep in mind shipping costs as well as the difficulty of shipping something big and potentially heavy. Regional brands can be just as popular, or even more so, due to their rarity, than the big national brands that everyone has heard of. One thing you will need to be on the lookout for with old advertising is knockoffs and reproductions, as there are a lot out there.

Barware

Another item that has some man-cave appeal is old barware. This can include old bar signs, bar trays, liquor jugs and decanters, and coasters. As with advertising, a lot of regional beers and liquors, including some that may be no longer produced, can be just as valuable as the big national brands. I've found barware stuff pretty much everywhere, and the prices I've seen folks asking for it are all over the map. I've bought beer trays for one to two dollars apiece at yard sales, seen those same trays being sold at thrift stores for five dollars and up, and seen trays sell for way too much money at auctions. So, like vintage advertising, barware's something you want to pick up if the price is right.

Souvenirs

I'm pretty partial to the souvenir style. I have a hard time passing up souvenirs when I come across them, and I do find them all over the place. Souvenirs appeal to shoppers who, like me, are drawn to that tacky vintage stuff, but they also appeal to people who want memorabilia from a specific place, whether it's a place where they live or a place where they made some happy memories. Old felt pennants are a popular souvenir item and, depending on size, age, and condition, can be worth from eight to twenty dollars apiece. Some other souvenirs to be on the lookout for include paperweights, letter openers, and T-shirts. But there are a whole host of tourist-shop tchotchkes out there. The nice thing about most souvenirs is that they are a breeze to ship and usually easy to store as well. After all, such items were designed to be easily packed in a suitcase.

Figurines

Most figurines will not be hugely valuable items, but they have proven to be reliable steady sellers for me. They don't cost too much to ship, and this tends to appeal to shoppers. If you want to add a vintage touch to your room or bookshelf, a vintage figurine is a nice, affordable way to do so. There are also shoppers who are always on the lookout for things such as particular types of animals or styles of figurines. At the low end, figurines sell for five dollars each, and at the high end, certain name-brand figurines can fetch thirty dollars or more. They are one of those items that you will find everywhere you go. I would never advise paying more than a dollar for a figurine when you are sourcing unless it happens to be a brand that routinely sells for a lot of money. I've bought whole lots of twenty or more figurines at auctions for a dollar, so I'm not inclined to pay too much for these little guys unless I think a particular figurine is especially cool looking.

However, I have been known to make exceptions to this rule. When I came across a whole collection of Beatrix

Potter figurines at a rummage sale for five dollars each, I bought them up. It helped that I had sold some of the same or similar figurines in the past and knew they would sell for between twenty and thirty dollars each on Etsy.

Because they are very breakable, it's always a good idea to examine figurines before making a purchase to make sure they are free of chips or cracks, including some that might have been repaired with glue. Although they can still be sold in slightly damaged condition, this will decrease their value.

Sets of Items

Certain types of collectibles might have been issued as a series, including different figurines, thimbles, or Christmas ornaments. A lot of these "collector's sets" issued by places such as the Franklin Mint and elsewhere are not especially valuable. So before snatching up these items, you might want to do a little research to see what the going rate for the set is. That said, some of these sets might appeal to collectors who are looking for an instant collection.

You can also create your own collector's sets if you're so inclined by putting together various similar collectible items together in a lot. This is especially useful for smaller, less valuable items that might not be worth selling individually.

Holiday Items

There's good money to be made with old holiday decorations, and you would be surprised how this stuff sells all year long. Of course, there's definitely an uptick in sales right before the approaching holiday. Christmas is by far the biggest holiday in terms of decorations and tchotchkes, and Christmas stuff really does sell all year long. But holidays such as Easter, Halloween, Valentine's Day, and Saint Patrick's Day also have a lot of decorations to accompany them. Old Halloween decorations, as well as old Halloween costumes, tend to be particularly valued by collectors, and even when you find such collectibles and the price is on the high side, you will still probably be able to earn a tidy profit. I find a lot of vintage holiday stuff at rummage sales as well as auctions, yard sales, and thrift stores. Thrift stores, like retail stores, tend to put out their holiday items just before a particular holiday approaches. This might make it difficult for online sellers, who won't have enough time to get an item listed before the ideal selling window has passed. But keep in mind, there's always next year. Oh, and just like retail stores, many thrift stores will mark down holiday items just after the holiday. This is a good time to snag some vintage holiday stuff at a discounted price.

Craft Kits and Patterns

Since Etsy got its start as a place for artists and artisans to sell their creations, the website counts a large number of crafters among its regular users. So it should come as no surprise that vintage craft kits and vintage sewing patterns do especially well on Etsy.

I love things like vintage embroidery and needlecraft kits, which I can often pick up for anywhere from one to four dollars at thrift stores and rummage sales and sell on Etsy for fifteen to twenty-five dollars, depending on condition, size, and design. I prefer to get these kits in sealed or new old-stock condition, as then I know that all the necessary components to complete the project are there. Items that list a designer's name on the package tend to be a little more desirable than packages that list only a manufacturer, but all of these kits tend to be good Etsy sellers and can be easily shipped.

Though less common, I've also come across other vintage craft kits over the years that have gone on to sell at nice profits in my Etsy shop. These include kits to make different miniatures, kits to make handbags, and kits to make stuffed animals, including printed cut-and-sew fabric panels.

Sewing patterns may not sell for a large amount of money. I generally sell vintage sewing patterns for six dollars, but since they can often be picked up very inexpensively, this makes for a nice profit. Most of the sewing patterns you will find will have been used with cut-out pattern pieces. These are still perfectly usable, provided all the pieces are still there and are in good condition.

Thankfully, most sewing patterns clearly indicate the number of pattern pieces and have numbers printed on each piece to make it easy to check for any missing pieces. When listing these items for sale, you'll want to make sure to include not only the size indicated on the pattern, but also the body measurements that correspond to that size, since sizes have changed a lot over the years.

Vintage craft supplies also have a big market of interested buyers on Etsy, some of whom may be using the materials to make their own items to sell on Etsy. Vintage buttons and other findings can often be grouped into lots for a quick sale, though you can also sell such items in smaller sets. I've done well selling vintage fabric that I've picked up at garage sales, rummage sales, and thrift stores on Etsy. The more interesting or distinctive the design of the material is, the better it seems to do. So prints that feature cute animals or particular objects, such as trains, have sold quickly on Etsy. Since crafters looking for fabric often need a specific amount of material, make sure to list the measurements for the piece you are selling.

This is a by no means exhaustive list of vintage items that you can sell on Etsy. Whether you choose to specialize in a particular type or style of item or take a more general approach to stocking your Etsy store's virtual shelves, you'll probably come across some of your own favorite items to sell.

Chapter 4
Listing Items

While at first glance the listing screen on Etsy may look complicated, it's relatively easy to master. Once you've listed a few items, you'll become comfortable with the page and creating new listings. The listings page has a number of different sections. First you need to upload photos of your item. Next you'll create a title for your listing, and then you need to classify your item by indicating how old it is and what category it fits in. After that you'll write a description of your item. You can select your shop sections. The next step is to set the shipping costs. And then you'll create thirteen tags to help shoppers find your item and then indicate any intended recipients or whether it's intended for a specific holiday or is typical of a certain style. It's a lot of information, but once you get a system going, it will take only a few minutes to create each listing.

Photos

I can't stress enough how hugely important good product photos are on Etsy. If you've sold elsewhere online, then you probably have some familiarity with taking pictures of your items. But unlike other sites, Etsy puts an emphasis on photos in listings and search, and Etsy shoppers have come to expect professional-looking product photos. The best product photos will look like something that could easily appear in a printed catalog. If your Etsy photos are subpar, it could negatively impact your sales. Not having good photos means shoppers might pass over your items in search, which means your items are less likely to be selected for Etsy treasuries, and in the long run, shoppers may be less inclined to purchase your items.

If you've spent any time on Etsy, whether it is browsing the home page, searching for different items, or looking at the shops of other sellers, you've likely seen how big a role photos play on Etsy. You've also probably noticed that some product photos look very appealing, while others look a bit amateur. Naturally, your goal should be to make your photos look as good as you possibly can.

The first step in taking a good product photo is your background. It should go without saying that photos taken on a messy table or an unmade bed are a bad idea. You want your item to be clearly visible, and to do that, you need a clean, uncluttered background. What background you choose will depend on your own personal preferences. Take a look at photos of different items on Etsy to see which backgrounds most appeal to you.

For my product photos, I generally use a clean white background. For the vast majority of my items, this allows them to stand out. White backgrounds are readily available and are easy to work with when editing photos. There are a number of ways to employ a clean white background, and some of them don't require a big investment.

One of my favorite sources of getting a white background is white foam board, which can be picked up at your local office supply store. It's cheap and easy to work with. For relatively flat items, it's easy to lay the foam board on a desk or table in a well-lit space, place my item on the board, and snap some pictures. You can even use foam board to take pictures of larger, three-dimensional items by using two pieces of foam board and propping one up against a wall and laying the other down on an adjacent table or desk. I've also used things such as plain white wrapping paper or even a shelf that's painted white to take photos.

If you want to upgrade to more professional equipment, photo cubes or tents are readily available, and, with the right lighting, they will allow you to take nice, clean photos of your products. They come in various sizes, so you'll probably want a size big enough to accommodate your largest items. By the way, even though I use a photo cube for my three-dimensional items, I still use my white foam board for taking pictures of flat items. It's simply very easy to use and gives me the best results.

The only time a white background will give you issues is when you are taking pictures of an item that itself is white and will get lost against the background. For these items you'll want to switch things up some. While a black background might be too stark a contrast with the white, a subtler but darker background usually does the trick. When I have a small white item to take a picture of, I usually set up a worn wooden box in my photo cube and then take a picture of the item with this box as backdrop. The weathered wood provides a soft but contrasting background that allows my item to stand out.

A background is only the first step in taking good photos of your items for Etsy. You'll also need good lighting. Far and away, the best lighting for product photos is natural sunlight, and that's something you can have for free. One drawback to sunlight is that you are dependent on the weather and the time of the day. It might get to the point where you find yourself planning your schedule around when they are predicting a sunny day. (Guilty as charged!) You don't need to be outside to take advantage of sunlight for lighting your photos. Provided you have some decently positioned windows in your home, you can easily use sunlight to light your photos.

When using sunlight you want a bright area, but you don't want to take pictures of your items in direct sunlight. This will create weird shadows and cause your photos to look washed out. When you see a puddle of light on the floor, that's the spot to avoid when setting up your photo area. Chances are it will take some experimentation to determine where in your home and what time of day will give you the best results. Keep in mind that as the seasons change, so too does the best time of day for taking photos.

High-quality photo lighting can also be used to light your photos, but note that if you are only using artificial lighting, you will need a number of lights to get a good photo. I like to use a pair of LED photo lights to supplement the natural light I use to take pictures using a photo cube. One thing you want to avoid when taking product photos is using the flash on your camera. It will lead to shadow and reflections and will give your photos an unnatural look.

Speaking of flashes, what sort of camera you use can make a difference in the quality of your photos, but don't assume that you need to invest hundreds of dollars in a new camera to take pictures of your Etsy items. A high-quality digital camera, probably something that you can purchase new for about $150 to $200, is probably plenty good enough to take good photos for Etsy. But also keep in mind if you have a smartphone that's a couple of years old or newer, it likely can take photos that are just as good as anything a decent digital camera can take and will work fine for taking Etsy photos. The only problem you may run into here is memory space, especially if you intend to take a big batch of photos at once.

Taking photos is only the first step in getting your photos ready for posting on Etsy. Even with the best lighting and a clean white backdrop, chances are your photos are still going to look a bit dark and nothing like the sort of thing you would expect to find in a professional catalog. You'll also find that the rectangle shape that all camera photos default to isn't in harmony with Etsy's square thumbnails. Don't worry; that's where editing comes into play.

I've read some advice that suggests you need expensive photo editing software such as Photoshop in order to edit photos for Etsy or other online sites. This simply isn't true. While Photoshop is a great product, it's designed for use by professional photographers and graphic designers who need to do a lot of complicated retouching, and you don't really need to do anything all that fancy. If you already have Photoshop or another high-end photo editing suite and are comfortable using it, by all means use it to edit your Etsy photos. If not, know that the plain old photo editing software that comes preinstalled on most computers works fine for getting your photos ready for Etsy.

On my Mac I use iPhoto to edit my pictures, and I know a similar simple program is available on PCs. All you need your software to be able to do is crop, lighten, and occasionally retouch. Cropping is pretty simple. You want to crop so that your item is front and center. You also want to make sure the photo that you'll be using as your first photo or main photo is more or less a square shape, and that's because this is how it will be displayed across the Etsy site, including in searches. If a photo is not already square, it will be cropped to a square shape in the display, and shoppers might not see the whole image. While you can crop all your photos to a square shape, you don't have to. Even though the preview will show as a square, when buyers click on each photo, it will load to its normal dimensions on the screen.

Lightening up photos is the key to making your images look bright, clean, and professional. You want your background to look nice, bright, and white (provided you're using a white background, that is), and you want your item to stand out clearly against the background and for the colors to look as close as possible to how they look in real life. If you overdo it on the lightening, your photo will start to look washed out and the detail will get lost. So it's a fine balance between too dark and too light, but with some practice and experimentation, you should be able to get it just right.

Retouching is necessary only if you have dirt spots or shadows on your background that don't disappear when you lighten your photo. Usually this is the result of a dirty background. (Once again, guilty as charged.) There should be no need to retouch your item when editing your photos.

Etsy allows you to post five photos with your listing. When taking photos, you'll probably want to snap a few more than this, since some of them will likely not come out perfectly and will be discarded. Your main image should be a clear shot of your object. After this you want to have some pictures from some different angles or perspectives—perhaps the back of an object or underneath it. You'll want at least one photo that shows size relevance. I use a fake apple for this in my photos or sometimes simply hold items with my hand. I've seen others use things such as coins or a ruler to show this as well. With most items you'll want a nice close-up photo, and if there is any damage, you should take a photo that shows this—and, of course, also be sure to mention it in your description.

Photos are a very important component of Etsy listings, but once you get comfortable taking and editing product photos, the process will become very simple, and, other than having to wait for a perfect sunny day, especially during the cold, gray winter season, it shouldn't give you many problems at all.

Titles

The title is the name that appears just under your product photos in an Etsy search and in your shop page. Titles should be written in mixed lowercase and capital letters, like book titles. You have 140 characters to write a title, which gives you room to be pretty detailed and specific in your title. Those who have sold on eBay know that the auction site limits titles to 80 characters. So Etsy's 140 characters is pretty generous. Because you have 140 characters to work with, you probably shouldn't resort to many abbreviations. You'll need to think in terms of the words someone might use to search for a particular item. If it's a very common abbreviation, such as a state postal abbreviation or a common nickname for an object such as hankie as opposed to handkerchief, then it would make sense to include it in your listing's title. But otherwise, keep your use of abbreviations to a minimum.

When creating titles it's a good idea to lead with the words a seller is most likely to use to search for your item. In most cases these are going to be the words that say exactly what your item is, such as "Portable Record Player," "Rainbow Stripe Polaroid Camera," or "Seahorses Print Handkerchief." Then follow this up with more words that help to describe the item, including words that describe its age (even if it's just the term "vintage"), size, color, or other pertinent details.

Why are the first words of your title so important? Two reasons. First of all, when you look at an Etsy search or at your shop page, the titles get truncated. Shoppers see only the first few words of your title. They need to click through to the listing to see the full title. The other reason the first words of titles matter more than the other words has to do with the way search engines such as Google determine what a page is about and if it is relevant for someone doing an Internet search. Google looks at the first few words in a page's title—in this case your listing's title—to see what the page is about. So leading with the words that best identify your item will help your listing to be displayed higher in Google searches.

While you will also classify your item as vintage using Etsy's dropdown menus, it's still a good idea to include the word "vintage" (or "antique" for items a hundred or more years old) in your title as well. Because Etsy is a marketplace for both handmade and vintage items, I like to be clear and upfront with shoppers about what my item is, and including this in the title might help to clear up confusion.

Categories

Etsy uses a series of dropdown menus to help you classify your product. In the first set of boxes, Etsy is looking for information to determine if the item is a handmade or vintage. And if it's vintage, they want a rough idea of when it dates from—a decade for twentieth-century items or a century for older items. You'll know exactly when some items are from because there is a date printed on the item or packaging. This is often true of things such as books and toys. With other items, the style (especially with clothing and accessory items) can be a pretty good indicator of about when your item is from. Beyond this, if you're not sure you'll have to do some research to see if you can determine when your item is from or give your best estimate of when you think it's from. If you're estimating the date, you may want to indicate this in your description below, perhaps providing some explanation for how you came to this conclusion.

Next it's time to classify your item by what category best suits it. Etsy has added a lot of different subcategories to the site, but even so you might find yourself with an item that doesn't fit neatly into any specific category. Do your best at selecting the most appropriate category. Note that you don't have to make a selection from each subcategory list. That is, if you've classified your item as belonging to the toys and games category and selected toy from the next menu, but can't find a selection that matches your item on the toy subcategory listing, you don't need to make one and can simply leave the cursor over the "select category" field.

While it is best to take the time to select the category that best matches your item, you don't need to spend a lot of time on this and shouldn't spend much time worrying if you are unable to locate a category section to match your item exactly. The category sections probably won't be driving much traffic or sales to your items. They help to determine where your item appears in Etsy's browse sections, and when a shopper does a search on Etsy that returns a lot of results, he or she can use the categories to help narrow down the selection. With vintage items, I've found that most people find my shop by looking for very specific items and the category selections play little to no role in their locating my wares.

Pricing Items

A subscriber to my YouTube channel once asked for my insights into the art of pricing items on Etsy, and that made me wonder if there an art involved in pricing Etsy items. I'd never really thought about it that way before, but she might be onto something there.

If I'm listing an item that's similar to something I've sold before or is something I sell on a regular basis, then I probably already know the listing price. For example, I generally sell sewing patterns for six dollars. To me this is a fair price for what I've paid for them, and it seems to be a price that buyers are willing to pay, as they sell on a regular basis.

But with most of the items I sell, some research is involved in determining how much I will price the item for. The easiest way to research the selling price for a vintage item is to simply do an Etsy search for it. Do any other sellers have the same item or a similar item for sale? What is their asking price? Oftentimes you can find the same item being sold by multiple sellers. While sometimes the prices are pretty comparable, oftentimes you will notice that the prices seem to be all over the map. When you are using other listings as a reference, do take into account the condition of the different items (some vintage items might be in much worse shape than the item you are selling), and also note what the seller's shipping costs are. As for setting your own price, you probably want to look for a price that's somewhere in the middle of what other sellers have it listed for. On Etsy, there's no need to have the lowest price, and in some cases, buyers may worry about the condition of an item is if the price seems too low. You also don't want to shortchange yourself. You want to be able to make a nice profit after your fees and the cost you paid to purchase the item are taken into consideration.

You will run into times when you simply cannot find anyone else on Etsy selling a particular item. In that case, you will have to take your search elsewhere. eBay is the next obvious place for checking prices. When researching prices on eBay, I would recommend searching only for sold, completed listings. People can and do list items for any price they feel like on eBay, but this doesn't always reflect the price that someone will actually pay. Because eBay tends to be the bargain basement of the Internet, I would definitely not recommend using the lowest price on eBay. In fact, when using eBay as a research tool, the higher seller prices are usually the best indicator of an item's actual value.

When you cannot find an item on Etsy or eBay, it's probably somewhat rare and therefore likely has some value to it. You might try a Google search to see if you can find any information on the value of the item. You can also check to see if your local library has any resources that can help you estimate the value or see if anyone on Etsy's forums or other public forums has any expertise on the subject.

Occasionally when conducting Google searches for a particular item, you might come across sold items on Etsy. You'll notice on these "sold" pages that there is no price information. It's perfectly okay to send a conversation to the Etsy seller to ask what the item sold for. I've received such questions from time to time and am always happy to provide such information to fellow sellers.

One thing to keep in mind when setting your prices is that some buyers may contact you wondering if your price is negotiable and if you would be willing to accept less for the item. Unlike on eBay, where the "best offers" I've received tend to be absurdly low, most Etsy shoppers are very reasonable in their offers. While you are under no obligation to accept offers, if you think this is something you might be open to, consider this when setting the selling price of your item. You should probably select a price that's a little bit higher than the absolute minimum that you would be willing to accept. You might also want to use coupon codes or put items in your shop on sale at some point, and if so, you will then be discounting your asking price on items—another reason to never set your selling price as the lowest you would be willing to accept.

Descriptions

Your description offers you a chance to give more detailed information about the item you are selling. Etsy shoppers have come to expect a well-written and thorough description, so you don't want to skimp on your details. Another reason you don't want to skimp on details is that the information you include in your description will, along with the first few words of your title, determine how your listing shows up in Google and other searches. In addition to the page's title, Google will examine the content of the page to see how well it matches what is in the title. So, while you don't want to be too repetitive, it will help your search engine optimization, or SEO, if you reuse the keywords from your title and mix things up a bit by using synonyms or different versions of words. Selling a rotary phone? Use the word "phone" a few times in your description, but also try using the word "telephone."

What sort of information should your description include? First of all you want to explain exactly what your item is. This may mean repeating some of the information already in your title. That's okay. Be as specific as you can be in describing your item. Explain when or about when the item is from. Did you learn any interesting facts when researching this item? Share them here. Is there an interesting story about the item's provenance? Maybe you picked it up from someone who collected such things, or perhaps it belonged to the grandmother of the person who sold it to you. You don't need to include such information, but including it can make items more appealing to Etsy buyers who are as much interested in the history of the item as they are in the item itself. The fact is, you won't know much about the provenance of most of the items you acquire, so when you do learn such details, it's nice to include them.

One rule of thumb that I try to use when describing my items is to write a description as if the person cannot see what the item looks like. Yes, you have taken and posted five nice, clear photos to accompany your listing, but not everyone is visual. So creating a word picture to accompany the actual pictures can go along way toward making someone on the other side of the computer screen acquainted with your product. It also helps those who are searching via Google or Etsy to find it, since the software will pick up on those descriptive words and deliver up your listing as a relevant search result.

In your description make sure to include any flaws or damage that your item has. Once again, though you will try to take photos of such issues, you also want buyers to clearly know what condition an item is in. If it's in like-new condition, note that, but keep in mind that buyers don't expect vintage items to be perfect. So giving them a clear description of any flaws usually won't scare them away from buying your item.

It's also a good idea to give the measurements of any item you are selling, whether it's an article of clothing or a coffee mug. Once again, you've taken a picture to show size relevance, but some buyers prefer to see a clear measurement of just how big or small an item is. So keep a measuring tape handy when writing your item descriptions.

Shop Sections

When you first start up your shop, you might not see the need for creating different shop sections. After all, you've only got a few items listed for sale. But as you add more and more items to your inventory, you'll see that shop sections help to organize your wares and make it easy for shoppers to find your items. What shop sections you use will depend on the types of items you sell. For example, someone who sells mostly clothing may have different sections for different types of garments or different styles of clothes, while a seller like me, who doesn't sell much clothing, may only have a single section devoted to clothing and accessory items. You can always go back and change the shop sections that you are using, but in some cases this will mean you need to change the section for certain items. This is something that can be done in bulk, so even that is not that much work.

When creating a listing, don't forget to select the shop section from the drop-down menu just below the description. The choices will be the different store sections you have created. One thing to keep in mind: when someone clicks on one of your listings, Etsy will display what they've identified as related items from your shop in the sidebar. These are items from the same shop section. This is one more reason to pay attention to how you use shop sections.

Shipping Costs

If you take the time to set up shipping profiles for your shop (see Chapter 5 for more on this), then setting the shipping prices when creating your listings will be super easy. All you will need to do is select the shipping profile from the drop-down menus that seems most appropriate for your item's size and weight. Even if you use shipping profiles, you can modify shipping costs for some nonstandard items. For example, on some less expensive items, you might want to lower your domestic shipping cost, even though in some cases this might mean you will have to eat some of that cost. If you feel this will still give you enough of a profit, by all means go ahead and do it. And by unlinking your shipping costs, you can easily change the shipping charge for one or more destinations on an item's listing without having to start from scratch with setting the shipping costs and without having to create a new shipping profile.

Tags

Tags are one of the most important parts of an Etsy listing, and for some reason many sellers skip over this section or don't fully use tags to their advantage. Tags are the keywords that Etsy uses to determine how relevant your item is for folks searching for items on Etsy. Most of the folks who view my shop and the items in it have found it due to Etsy searches. Based on the tags I use, Etsy will display my item in the searches that different shoppers perform.

Etsy allows you to use thirteen tags to identify your item, and it should be your goal to use every single one of them. Obviously you'll want to use tags that describe what your item is. Selling a rotary telephone? You'll be using tags such as "rotary telephone," "vintage phone," "old-fashioned phone," and so on. Does the phone work? You'll probably want to include "works" and "working" as keywords. What about color? Let's say it's "yellow," but what sort of yellow? Maybe you want to include "bright" or "lemon," depending on the shade. Don't forget to include the word "vintage" and maybe even "retro." Be creative but accurate when choosing tags for your listing.

It's a good idea to look at your Etsy shop stats on a regular basis. This will allow you to see how many people are visiting your shop, but you'll also be able to see other details as well, including which of your listings receive the most traffic and what search terms have brought Etsy searchers to your listings. Checking these stats on a regular basis will give you an idea of which of your keywords work well and will give you a glimpse into the sort of buyers interested in what you have to sell.

Style, Recipient, and Occasion

Etsy also provides you with drop-down menus where you can identify the intended recipient of the item as well as the relevant style or styles that describe the item. You do not need to use these drop-down menus, but if your item clearly has an intended audience or a specific style, including this information will help shoppers find your item. The choices you make from these menus will determine how your item will appear when someone is using Etsy's browse function.

For example, if you have something that's clearly a men's accessory item, such as a pair of vintage cufflinks, you'll want to select "men" from the "Who is it for?" menu, while something like pink flowered stationery is most likely going to be intended for women. The style section is where you can highlight one or two styles that describe the nature of your item and includes things such as Art Deco and Mid Century. So, if you have an item that is clearly of a particular style, this is a good place to indicate that. Note that a lot of the items you list probably won't have a single intended recipient or a clearly defined style.

Though less common, you may also wish to include the occasion that the item is suitable for. This would most likely be for something such as a holiday decoration or a greeting card that celebrates a specific holiday or milestone. Etsy's drop-down menu gives a list of several holidays and milestone events to choose from.

Relisting Items

When you list an item in your Etsy shop, it gets listed for four months, but after those four months, the listing expires. In most cases, you will want to renew these listings. You can find your expired listings under the Listings Manager. While you can bulk relist expired listings using the check boxes, I would not recommend doing this for two reasons. First of all, you may want to take a look at any unsold items to see if there is anything you can do to tweak your listing. Are there any glaring spelling errors that might confuse buyers or prevent them from easily finding your listing? Are the photos of good quality? How about the description? Could it be rewritten in any way to be clearer or more appealing? Is your price reasonable? I don't think there's any reason to drop the price on something that hasn't sold in four months, but after eight months, you might want to consider lowering the price on an item. It may not be necessary, but it's one thing to look into.

The second reason I would advise against bulk relisting is that it isn't going to be a huge benefit to you in terms of driving traffic to your shop, because the newest items show up toward the top of searches. You will get more traffic if you have recently listed or relisted items. However, because of this, I think it's to your benefit to relist or list a few items at a time and to spread this out during the course of the day and the course of the week. It's much more beneficial to you in terms of traffic to list or relist a few items each day than to list or relist a whole batch of items on a single day.

Creating a System

One way to streamline the process of listing items on Etsy and to become more efficient is to create a system for listing items. Rather than writing listings and taking photos on an item-by-item basis, you can batch things to save yourself time.

I write out the titles and descriptions for my items and identify the shipping profile I will use before I list my items. I use a standard spiral notebook to write all this information down and usually will write up a batch of listings while watching television to make it a little more fun. Of course, I would probably get more listings written per hour if I didn't have the television distraction, but this lets me keep up with some shows I like to watch without feeling I'm goofing off in front of the TV. So it's sort of a win-win situation for me.

Once I've written up the description for an item, I move it to my "to be photographed" pile. Then, once I have some time and a nice sunny day, I get my photo area set up and take pictures of a batch of Etsy items. Although I upload all my photos to my computer right away, I usually don't bother editing individual photos until right before I list the item. There's no real reason for this other than the fact that editing photos is somewhat tedious and I prefer not to edit a whole batch of photos at once.

As for listing items, I'll usually try to list three or four items at a time and have a goal (that I don't always meet!) of listing or relisting twelve items each day. When I sit down to list my items, I get out my trusty notebook and tear out the pages for the items I plan on listing. In some cases, I've already determined the price I'll be listing the item for. Usually this is with items that I sell on a regular basis. With items I want to research the price for, I'll go ahead and do some research on Etsy, eBay, and elsewhere to determine the best price and mark this down on my written-out listing. Finally, I go about creating my listings on Etsy using the photos that I've just edited and the information that I wrote down on my notebook page.

With this system, I have a better shot at meeting my twelve-items-a-day goal. Because I have already done most of the work ahead of time, there isn't too much I have to do when it comes time to create the listing, and that means I'm less likely to put off listing things until I have more time or am less tired—excuses I have definitely used in the past when I simply tried writing the descriptions and titles at the same time that I was creating the listings on Etsy.

My advice is to find some sort of system that works for you. It doesn't have to be the same as my system, of course. Your goal should be to find a way to be as efficient with creating listings as you are able to, and a system will almost always improve your efficiency.

Chapter 5
Shipping

Probably one of the biggest concerns for new sellers is shipping out items. Sellers are confused by postal pricing, aren't sure how much items weigh, or perhaps simply fear having to stand in line at the post office. On the flip side are those sellers who aren't concerned about shipping until they've made a few sales and learned that they grossly underestimated shipping costs to the point where they find they are losing money on each sale. Shipping doesn't need to be scary, though. Once you've familiarized yourself with the process, it's quite painless.

Shipping Methods

US sellers, for the most part, will probably be shipping items via the US Postal Service. The exception might be especially large or heavy items, where your best bet may be UPS. For especially large items, such as pieces of furniture, you'll probably need to work with a freight company. Chances are, though, if you're just getting started on Etsy, you'll begin with items that are a little easier to ship, than, say, a four-poster bed.

The US Postal Service has a number of breakdowns for mail services, but there are three main ways you'll most likely be shipping out your Etsy packages, and which service you use will be determined by weight. (A fourth service, Media Mail, is available for books. It's significantly cheaper than Priority Mail or Standard Mail [aka Parcel Post], so this may be how you want to ship larger sets or lots of books. You should make it clear in the listing that the books will be shipped via Media Mail, and you should warn buyers that this service is significantly slower than regular shipping methods. Because it can take more than a week for Media Mail packages to reach most destinations, I would not use it for smaller collections of books and would instead offer shipment via Priority Mail.)

Any Etsy package that weighs less than one pound can be shipped via First Class Mail. This is the least expensive shipping method offered by the US Postal Service. In general this will be for items that fit neatly in a bubble mailer or a small box. The post office requires you to use your own packaging material for First Class packages. This means you should be thinking about the cost of these materials when setting the item price or shipping cost for your item. Since the post office is fond of raising rates, I won't include a current rate table, as it will likely be outdated quickly. When looking into First Class postage rates, make sure you look at the rate for nonmachinable mail or small packages. This will cost more than mailing machinable mail, a.k.a. things such as letters and postcards. One thing that makes First Class Mail easy for new sellers to figure out is that the rates are flat. That is, whether you are mailing a First Class package to a state next door or to a state all the way on the other side of the country, the rate will be the same. First Class packages usually take anywhere from a few days to a week to arrive.

Packages that weigh more than a pound will most likely be shipped via Priority Mail, though if they are extra heavy, you may want to consider Standard Post. More on that in a bit. Unlike First Class Mail, Priority Mail prices vary by zone. The only exception to that is the Flat Rate Priority Mail boxes that the post office provides. Currently they offer different sizes of flat-rate envelopes, a small flat-rate box, two different medium flat-rate boxes, and two different large flat-rate boxes. These flat-rate packages can help take the guesswork out of figuring out how much it will cost to ship an item, since the rate is the same no matter how much the item weighs or where it is going. But with the medium and large flat-rate boxes, the rate is high, and unless the item is over three pounds, it will probably cost less to ship it in a non-flat-rate box or a regional-rate box. The regional-rate boxes are similar to the flat-rate boxes in that the price is the same regardless of weight, but the price will vary depending on where the item is going. That is, if a regional-rate package is going to your own state or a neighboring state, the rate will be lower than if it is going to a destination several states away, while with any Priority Mail package that is neither a flat rate nor a regional rate, both destination and weight will determine the cost.

One nice thing about Priority Mail is that the post office supplies free boxes and envelopes for shipping Priority Mail packages. You can pick them up at your local post office or order them in quantity from USPS.com and have them delivered to your door at no charge. You'll still need to supply your own padding, void fill, and tape, so those costs should be figured into determining your prices. Most Priority Mail packages take two to three days to arrive at their destination. Tracking and insurance is included with all Priority Mail packages.

For larger, heavier items, Standard Post (it used to be called Parcel Post) will probably be your most economical option, though it does depend on where an item is headed to. With packages headed to a destination in your own region—for example, a neighboring state—you can usually get a cheaper rate shipping Priority Mail as opposed to Standard Post. As with First Class packages, the post office requires you to use your own packaging when shipping items via Standard Post. Standard Post packages take an estimated two to eight days to arrive and include tracking.

Calculated or Fixed Price?

Basically, Etsy offers sellers two ways of setting the shipping price. You can either take advantage of Etsy's calculated shipping tool to have your shipping price determined by the weight and size of your package and the buyer's location, or you can set a fixed shipping price of your own choosing. You can use a different fixed price with each item you list and you can set different prices for various international destinations, but you will not be able to change your fixed price depending on the buyer's location within the country. For US sellers with domestic shipments that use zoned-based pricing such as Priority Mail, there can be a significant difference in the shipping cost for a buyer in your own state versus a buyer on the other side of the country. Using a calculated option will allow you to charge a more accurate shipping price, but it may take a little longer to set the shipping price as you are listing each item.

Sellers coming from eBay may be comfortable with Etsy's calculated shipping option, which, though a little different from eBay's system, works in a similar way. Calculated shipping is also useful for new sellers who aren't yet familiar with the different post office rates. Using calculated shipping usually means you will need to weigh your items with any packaging material you will use (or know in advance a rough estimate of the weight of the packing material) before listing an item so that you can fill in this information on the listing page. It's an extra step, but it could save you a lot of money, especially if you are unsure of shipping costs.

Using Etsy's shipping profiles to create several different fixed-rate shipping charges can be a huge time-saver if you are planning to list a lot of items, but it means you will need to first familiarize yourself with all the rates charged by the US Post Office (or your preferred carrier), and it means you will need to become pretty good at estimating how much a packed-up item is going to weigh. The good news is that, as I can attest, one becomes skilled at estimating the shipping weight of items pretty quickly.

Combined Shipping Discounts

One way to encourage buyers to purchase multiple items is to offer a combined shipping discount for buyers who purchase more than one item. When you are creating a listing or setting up a shipping profile, this is the second box, with the column heading "With another item." What this means is that when a buyer purchases more than one item from you, he or she will only pay the full shipping price on the first item and the "With another item" charge will be added to this number to give the total combined shipping.

So let's say you have a mug that has a five-dollar shipping charge, and you have a set of salt and pepper shakers that also has a five-dollar shipping charge but with a two-dollar "With another item" shipping price. A buyer purchasing both the mug and the salt and pepper shakers would pay only seven dollars to have both items shipped instead of ten dollars. In most cases these will be items you'll be able to box up together, so it will cost you less money to mail out both items together than it would to send them separately.

You can set the "with another item" shipping price either when setting up a shipping profile or when listing an item. What you set it at will be determined by the size and weight of the item. For especially light items, something like a handkerchief or a greeting card, it might make sense to set the "With another item" price to zero.

International Shipping

A lot of sellers are scared when it comes to international shipping. In some ways their fears may be justified. International shipping can be quite pricey, and if you make a mistake in setting the international shipping price for your item and estimate it too low, you could stand to lose quite a bit of money. For new sellers just getting used to weighing items and calculating prices, getting the international shipping rate right may seem like a challenge. But once you get familiar with it, international shipping is not scary.

You are not required to offer international shipping, and you may decide to forgo it for now or forgo it for especially large and heavy items. But offering international shipping is something you probably want to set your sights on.

I'd say that roughly 10 percent of the items I sell in my Etsy shop are purchased by international buyers. Because not all sellers offer international shipping on their items, this means you'll have less competition for international orders. Plus, keep in mind that items that might be more common and less valuable domestically will be harder to come by, and thus worth more, in other countries.

When looking into international shipping, you'll notice that the post office offers two classes of international shipments: First Class Mail International and Priority Mail International, and while you might think these would correspond to domestic First Class and Priority Mail, that's not quite the case. While the rule with domestic First Class parcels is that they must be under one pound, with First Class International, the package only needs to be under three pounds. This is why most of my international shipments go via First Class Mail International. The rates are more affordable, but, as I said, they are still pretty steep. Priority Mail International, though, is extremely steep. One good thing about Priority Mail International is that you can use the same packaging that you use for your stateside Priority Mail packages, and there are even flat-rate options available for international shipments as well.

As you look into the prices for international shipments, you might notice that the shipping prices in many cases will be as high as or higher than your item price, and you might be discouraged from even bothering to add an international shipping option, since it might seem unlikely that a buyer would pay more to have an item shipped than that item is selling for. I assure you, that's not the case. Time and time again I've sold items that were going to foreign countries and the buyers paid more in shipping costs than they did to purchase the items. Those who purchase from international sellers are used to such fees, and if somebody wants something badly enough, he or she will pay dearly for it.

While you can calculate the shipping charges for each individual country, I would not recommend doing this. It takes a lot of time, and there's no real need for it. For all but my heaviest listings, I use a shipping profile that includes the domestic shipping price, the Canadian shipping price, and the blanket Everywhere Else shipping price. I separate out Canada because rates are a little bit lower for Canada-bound packages, and I would say that of my international sales, probably half are Canada. As I mentioned previously, I use Etsy's shipping profiles to save time when listing items and rely on a guesstimate of how much the shipping cost is going to be. For domestic items I use the mean price, but for international shipments, I generally use the most expensive. The difference between rates is far greater for international shipments, so you want to be wary about underestimating the cost to ship an item.

Often, international buyers contact me before making a purchase, and I am able to provide them with the actual shipping costs.

Should You Offer Free Shipping?

Free shipping is a big deal when it comes to purchasing items online. Amazon.com is famous for their free shipping, though it should be noted that this free shipping is provided to buyers who spend a minimum amount or who pay an annual fee for their Prime service. Also, the sheer number of packages that Amazon ships means they receive extraordinary shipping discounts from carriers. That said, it's true that online shoppers love to get free shipping.

There really is no such thing as free shipping. Any seller who's offering free shipping has built the cost of shipping into the purchase price of the item, unless he or she has goofed and made a mistake. So even though buyers are still technically paying for shipping, they still find the offer of free shipping enticing.

On sites such as eBay, offering free shipping can lead to higher search rankings and more buyers seeing your item, but at this time Etsy has no feature that allows shoppers to only see items with free shipping or to even display those items first in search results. In fact, on Etsy, making it clear to buyers that you offer free shipping means you have to include this information in your item's title and description. With this in mind, there isn't really a huge benefit to offering free shipping on Etsy.

There's also one small drawback to offering free shipping on Etsy: you will pay a little bit more in fees. This is because Etsy takes 3.5 percent of the selling cost of your item but doesn't take a percentage from your shipping charges. So by offering free shipping and rolling the cost of the shipping into your item price, you'll end up paying Etsy 3.5 percent on that shipping cost.

So, at present, it doesn't really make sense to offer free shipping as an Etsy seller, and most Etsy sellers do not offer free shipping.

Purchasing Postage on Etsy

The post office has taken steps to decrease lines at their service counters, and one of those measures is encouraging folks to purchase postage for their packages online and then drop them off or schedule a pickup. Their method for encouraging this is to offer significant discounts for purchasing postage online. Etsy sellers have the added of advantage of receiving additional discounts when using Etsy's built-in shipping tool.

With Etsy's own shipping option, postage fees will be automatically added to your current Etsy bill and you can print postage with the click of a button, without having to fill in address and shipping info. So, in addition to the money you save, you'll also save yourself some time. All postage purchased on Etsy includes a tracking number. You can set up your account to have this tracking number automatically e-mailed to customers when you print out your postage.

Thanks to Etsy's partnership with Endicia, it's easy for sellers to purchase and print postage directly from their Etsy accounts. This saves a lot of time, and since Etsy passes the discounts received from Endicia on to you, it can also save you a lot of money. You can purchase any USPS postage through Etsy, whether an item is going domestically or internationally. You won't need to install any special software, but you will need to have some sort of scale for weighing your packages. Any sort of postage scale can be used for this. The scale should be able to accurately measure packages to the ounce. It does not need to connect to your computer.

When purchasing postage directly through Etsy, you need only provide the package's weight and dimensions. The software then will show the cost, and once you agree to the charge, you can print out your label. There's no need to enter the buyer's shipping address. It will automatically print out on the label.

Although it's called a label, it can be printed on plain white paper, cut out, and affixed to your package using clear packing tape, though be sure to not tape over the bar code. If you wish to use labels, you will want the half-sheet-size labels, which come two to a sheet. Once you have attached your label to the package, you can either drop it off at your post office or schedule a pickup with your mail carrier. Please note that the zip code of your return address is the post office that your packages should be shipped out of.

Packing Materials

Your shipping arsenal should include a variety of plain cardboard boxes in different sizes perfect for First Class or Standard Mail shipments. You'll probably also want some padded mailers or bubble mailers. With mailers, you'll probably need to purchase such items new. When it comes to boxes, you may be able to recycle them. Depending on your volume of sales, you may want to ask friends and relatives to save boxes for you or make friends with some local businesses that regularly dispose of boxes. Avoid very beat-up or very marked-up boxes, as these don't look very professional, and beat-up boxes may not adequately protect your merchandise. Keep in mind that boxes that have been printed with liquor-company logos and information or with other liquid or hazardous material info cannot be mailed as is through the post office and probably shouldn't be used. While you can cover or cross out any such incriminating information, this will not make for an attractive presentation when your item arrives at the buyer's doorstep.

Recycled boxes aren't the only source of free supplies. The post office generously supplies anyone who asks with Priority Mail boxes and mailers and will deliver them to your door for free. The only drawback to these items is that they can *only* be used for Priority Mail shipments, but other than this, they are a fantastic free resource. You can place your orders for free boxes and mailers at USPS.com or check at your local post office to see if they have any that they would be willing to give you. One thing to note with Priority Mail boxes is that certain boxes are labeled "flat rate" or "regional rate." When purchasing postage for such boxes, you must purchase the flat-rate or regional-rate postage that corresponds to the box being used.

Packing material and void fill are essential to ensure that your item makes it to its destination in one piece. Padded mailers are designed for flat items—things such as greeting cards, books, and sewing patterns can be shipped safely and securely in a padded mailer, but if you are shipping any sort of three-dimensional object, you'll want to use a box and appropriate packing material.

Bubble wrap, tissue paper, newsprint, or bogus paper and air cushions are all examples of suitable packing material. What you use will depend on the item and the size of the box. For any sort of breakable item, I use Bubble Wrap. Sometimes, especially if it's a smaller, more delicate item such as a figurine, I will wrap it in a sheet of tissue paper first and then cover it with Bubble Wrap. But in many cases I still have some empty space in the box. You don't want this, as your item will then get knocked around in the box as it travels to its new home—plus, the box is more likely to become crushed in transit. In this case, some void fill will help to keep it securely in place. More Bubble Wrap or air pillows or cushions work well for this. You can also use recycled materials, including newsprint or kraft paper. One thing to keep in mind if you're using paper is that it weighs more than lighter packing materials such as Bubble Wrap and air cushions, and, depending on the shipping method you are using and where the item is going, it could significantly increase your shipping costs. Of course, if you are sending something in a flat-rate or regional-rate package, this extra weight will have no impact on your shipping costs.

Though once a staple of shippers, Styrofoam packing peanuts have fallen out of favor, most likely because they can be annoying to deal with, both for the seller and the buyer, who receives an item along with hundreds of annoying peanuts he or she must now dispose of. So you might want to avoid these in your packing.

Recycling bubble wrap, air cushions, and other packing material from packages you have received or packages others have received is a great way to cut down on the costs of shipping your items. Some enterprising sellers have even been known to raid the Dumpsters behind stores for boxes and packing material. (Please note if you plan on Dumpster diving for your packing supplies, you should first check to make sure it is legal in your area and should always wear rubberized work gloves and sturdy closed-toe shoes.) When using recycled material for shipping your packages, always make sure that it is in good and clean condition. When a buyer opens your package and finds dirty packing material, it sends the wrong message and will lead to an unhappy customer and a poor review.

What to Include in a Package

Besides your item, well packed to prevent any in-transit damage, what else should go into a package? Well, you aren't required to send anything else, but it's good practice to include a packing slip. This can be accomplished by either selecting the option to "print order" or "print gift receipt" when you are on the orders screen in Etsy. Since my computer and my items are not located in the same room, I also use these printouts to make sure I grab all the items I need to ship out when I am getting my shipments ready. I like to handwrite a simple thank-you message on each of these slips, though, of course, you aren't required to do so.

Please note: you can customize the information that appears when you select the option to "print order" on Etsy. An important piece of information that you may wish to exclude is the item price and shipping charges. Many buyers purchase items as gifts on Etsy and sometimes have them shipped directly to the recipients.

Some sellers like to include a small gift with each order, but, of course, you do not need to this. Since I'm also an author and have an excessive number of bookmarks and promotional stickers, I'll usually toss one of these into my package as well. If you have business cards for your Etsy shop, it's a good idea to include one, and, if you want, you can use the Etsy coupon codes promotional tool to create a discount for the buyer to use on a future order and include a print coupon with your package.

When and How Often to Ship Items

When you create a shipping profile on Etsy, you have the option of setting an expected shipping time. It's always safer to underestimate this. Although my practice is to ship daily Monday through Friday, I have my shipping time set as one to two business days. This is to protect myself in case circumstances arise that prevent me from shipping out packages on time. Perhaps something comes up that prevents me from getting to the post office on time. My Internet might be down, or the Etsy site might be experiencing problems. Or a storm or other event could knock out power. Although these are all unusual circumstances, they can arise, and I don't want to have upset customers if I can't, for any reason, ship out a package the next business day.

How often you ship out orders depends on your own situation. Are you able to make it to the post office each day or schedule a pickup? Does it make more sense for you to only ship out on certain days of the week? Whatever the case, you should be upfront with your customers about when and how often you ship out packages. If there are circumstances that will delay the shipment of packages, let your customers know this by sending an Etsy conversation.

Because you are running a business and because shoppers have come to expect items they order online to arrive quickly, it's best practice to ship out items as soon as you are able to. Your goal should be daily shipments. Ultimately, you want your buyers to be pleasantly surprised at how quickly a package arrives and not annoyed by how long it takes to get to them.

Shipping Upgrades

It's likely that most of the packages you ship out will be sent using Priority Mail or First Class Mail. Both are pretty speedy delivery services. This is plenty fast enough for most buyers to receive packages on time. However, there are always those buyers who have waited until the last minute or, due to unusual circumstances, need something very quickly and will ask if there's a way to pay extra to have a package sent to them quicker.

In most cases, when I tell these shoppers how soon the Priority Mail package is expected to arrive, this is fine. But in some cases, they are still interested in paying extra for an expedited shipment. In this case, I use the Express Mail option. It costs significantly more than Priority Mail, and, in most cases, the delivery time is about the same, with one exception. Express Mail shipments are guaranteed for the delivery date, while Priority Mail packages are merely expected by that date. There is a difference in how the two types of mail are handled by the post office, and that higher price does mean that the post office takes extra steps to ensure the speedy arrival of Express Mail shipments.

There are different ways to handle expedited shipping requests. One is to create an item listing for "Expedited Shipping," which buyers can add to an order. This gives you all the options of laying out the delivery-time specifications in the listing and means buyers can add this to an order without having to make a special request. But such an option works best if all of your items are roughly the same weight and size, something that's unlikely when you are selling vintage items. The other issue is that depending on your shop layout, shoppers may have trouble locating the "Expedited Shipping" listing or even understanding how to add this to an order.

Another way to handle expedited shipping is to include an "expedited" option when setting up your shipping profiles. When buyers are checking out, they will have the chance to opt for this premium service.

I sell a lot of items on Etsy, but only occasionally do I receive requests for expedited shipping. So for me it's easier to handle these on a case-by-case basis. For buyers who are interested in paying for Express Mail delivery, I will revise the shipping costs for the listing they are interested in and usually add the word "RESERVED" to the title of my listing for them.

By the way, most of my questions about shipping time come in December. Around the fifteenth or so, questions start coming in from buyers who want to know, if they order that day, whether the item will make it to them before Christmas. In December it's not a bad idea to familiarize yourself with the holiday shipping times that the post office has stated. Often in December your local post office will display helpful signage that indicates the date Priority Mail and First Class Mail shipments must be sent by in order to arrive by Christmas. You can usually find this information at USPS.com as well.

Chapter 6
Marketing

Marketing is one of those topics that I've found new sellers have a lot of questions about and perhaps place a little too much faith in. Of course, we all want the same thing: for buyers to find our shop and to purchase our items. In the case of paid marketing opportunities, those who tout their services make it sound as if their product or opportunity will deliver exactly what you want. Some have found success using paid marketing opportunities; others have come to the conclusion that any sales that such opportunities generate don't justify the cost of the service.

My Most Successful Marketing Strategy

I have used paid Etsy ads and even dabbled in a few other ways of marketing my Etsy shop in the past, all with little or no success. But one day while perusing my Etsy shop stats, I had an epiphany. Looking at the number of unique page views my shop received, I noticed two things. First, overwhelmingly, the biggest source of traffic for my Etsy shop was Etsy searches—that is, shoppers using the search box on Etsy to locate items they were looking for. Second, I noticed that the number-two source of traffic was my own listings. What this meant was a shopper looking at one item in my store (perhaps one he or she found via an Etsy search) then clicked on another item in the shop. So I realized that if the number-one source of traffic for me was Etsy searches and the number-two source was people clicking on another listing in my shop, then one guaranteed way to increase traffic and in turn sales was to list more items.

Etsy, more so than most other online sales venues, really is a numbers game. The Etsy shop format means that more listings really will increase the number of views your items receive, and when your views increase, your sales almost certainly increase as well. This is not exactly a free form of marketing, since it does cost twenty cents to create each listing, but it's certainly an affordable and effective form of marketing your shop.

Though it's not necessarily a form of marketing, another thing that goes a long way toward increasing the number of sales you receive is improving the quality of your listings. Photos are of huge importance on Etsy, and nice, clean, high-quality photos will sell more items. Thorough, well-written descriptions and appropriate tags are also keys to generating traffic and sales.

I would only look into other forms of marketing once I had a significant number of items listed in my store (I wouldn't waste my time paying for paid marketing if I had fewer than two hundred active listings) and had already taken steps to make sure the photos and item descriptions were the best that they could be.

Social Media Marketing

Etsy does make it pretty easy for sellers to promote their shops and items via social media. You can integrate your Facebook, Twitter, and Pinterest accounts with your Etsy shop. Each time you create a new listing, you have the option to share it with the press of a button to any or all of these social media feeds. Since this isn't very time consuming, it's an easy way to do a little marketing.

That said, do such forms of promotion help you to sell more items? Well, it will depend on the followers you have on each of these different sites. If you've built up a big following of folks who are interested in purchasing vintage items, then sharing your listings with those followers will likely lead to sales. But if your social media channels are more general or personal in nature, you may not see too many sales as a result of this sharing. So be mindful of the time you spend promoting your items on social media and the results of this promotion.

Until a short while ago, I would have told you that I never sold any items as a result of social media promotion, but now I have to say that is no longer true. As my Planet Alissa YouTube channel has grown, I've generated some Etsy sales as a result. In these cases, I wasn't specifically marketing my products, just putting out some instructional or informational videos for Etsy vintage sellers. Still, creating YouTube videos for the sole purpose of marketing your products would likely not be the wisest use of time and probably wouldn't be worth the effort.

As a rule, if you are spending more time marketing your shop than listing items and maintaining the shop, you probably need to scale back the marketing efforts.

Etsy Ads

Probably the easiest and most common way of using paid marketing to promote your Etsy shop is to use Etsy's advertising program. This works with Etsy's search page, and by paying to promote certain listings, you can make sure your item appears at the top of a search when an Etsy user types in search terms that you specify. Etsy searches display the newest listed or relisted items first, but the very first row of a search shows paid Etsy advertisements, denoted with a small "Ad" in the corner.

If you've listed your item in the past day or two, chances are it will automatically show up on the first page of a search, but the longer an item's been for sale, the further back in the search results it will be. Now, depending on the item and its specific qualities, there may not be many similar items on Etsy. But for more common items, your listing could get lost in the sea of listings. In such cases, a paid Etsy ad might make sense. So, for example, something like a pair of pink earrings will get buried quickly in the search results, but something like a Lake George souvenir pennant will probably remain on the first search page for quite a bit longer.

For those who sell handcrafted items on Etsy, where the competition is steep, paid ads are one way of making sure their items get seen. Because many vintage items are so unique, a paid ad might not really be necessary. If you want to experiment with Etsy ads, I would choose items for which the Etsy market is pretty saturated, that have been for sale for at least a week in your shop, and for which your asking price is high enough to justify the money you spend on advertising. I would also start off with a small advertising budget. Etsy charges you each time someone clicks on one of your ads, and you can set an advertising budget so that your ads will no longer be displayed after you reach this cap.

Etsy will show you the details of your advertising campaign at the bottom of your shop stats page, so you can easily see how well your ads are performing and how much traffic they've generated. Depending on how well these ads do and any sales that result from them, you may want to tweak your ads or modify your campaign, which you can do at any time.

Other Paid Advertising

Probably the second-most common form of paid advertising, after Etsy ads, are Google ads. Much like Etsy ads, Google ads are geared toward searches or recent search history. You can use a Google ad to promote a specific web page. It's up to you whether you want to promote your main shop page or a specific listing. You can create more than one ad if you want to try both approaches or want to promote multiple listings. You draft the language of the ad and specify the search terms you want it displayed for. Google's costs depend on the popularity of search terms. More specific terms are usually less expensive than broader search terms. Like Etsy, you can set a specific budget, and your ads will stop running when you've exhausted that budget. Like Etsy, it's a pay-for-clicks format, and you can track the performance through Google's Adwords interface.

Etsy runs its own Google search ads promoting the site and specific listings on the site. So even though I don't pay for my own Google ads, I receive a regular stream of visits that are the result of Etsy's own Google advertising. So it's not necessary to run your own Google ads, and it might not make sense to compete against Etsy for ad space when they are advertising on your behalf.

There are lots of other forms of paid advertising that you can do on the Internet, but their efficacy can be questionable. Nearly every social networking site out there now has opportunities to promote posts or products on their site, and while people do spend a lot of time on social networking sites, usually they are not using them for shopping. Unlike Google or Etsy search ads, which are targeted to people looking for specific items, most likely because they are looking to buy that particular item, social media ads are seen by people who may have no interest in shopping at all. While there is the chance that these ads will persuade someone to buy something they didn't even know they wanted to buy, the likelihood of this happening is slim.

Blogs and other websites often sell ad space on their sites. Such ads are usually reasonably priced, and, depending on the site's theme and target audience, it might be a good fit for your products. If it's a site, say, geared toward collectors of dolls and you happen to have a lot of vintage dolls for sale in your shop, then advertising on one of these sites might work well for you. In general you want to find sites that will attract shoppers of the types of items you sell. It will be up to you to see how much traffic such ads generate and whether or not this leads to an increase in sales, but if the advertising costs are reasonable, it might be worth trying.

Repeat Business

One form of marketing that seems to make good sense is to market to people who you know purchase vintage items online, and you already know people who do this because they've purchased items from you. As you know from shopping online, purchasing from an online store often lands you on a new e-mail mailing list, and you'll be subjected to weekly, sometimes daily promotional e-mails. You don't want to do this to your customers, but you can easily create a mailing list using a free service such as MailChimp.com and invite buyers to join the list either in your automatic e-mail confirmation of their order or in a note enclosed in the package.

Even if you don't want to go through the trouble of creating a mailing list, you can encourage repeat business by enclosing a business card or a coupon for a discount on a future order in all Etsy orders you ship out. Etsy allows you to easily create coupon codes for marketing your shop that can be set for a percentage off or specific dollar amount off. You can have Etsy automatically e-mail customers a thank-you coupon good for their next order, or you can go ahead and mail them hard-copy coupons with their orders. I prefer to include the coupon with the order, in part because I think it's a bit annoying to get e-mailed a coupon immediately after making a purchase. Customers aren't likely to make another purchase right away, but when you mail them a coupon, it encourages them to come back and take another look at your shop to see if you've added any new items.

You can easily make your own print coupons with your unique coupon code to include with each of your orders. I wouldn't spend a lot of money getting coupons printed out, since in my experience they don't generate a huge number of sales, but you can easily print out simple coupons on your own printer to send to your customers. For a more professional look, business cards are a perfect size for coupons, and you can often find great deals on them from different online printing services

Networking

Business cards are great for including with your shipments, but they can also be a great way of letting others know about what you do. If you happen to run across collectors and folks interested in vintage wares in your travels, which is very likely if you find yourself stalking auctions, rummage sales, and other treasure troves of vintage goods, it's a good idea to pass on your card to them. In most cases it won't lead to a sale, but you never know where this networking might lead. It also doesn't hurt to hand out your cards or multiple cards to friends or relatives who will gladly talk up your business. You might end up making some new connections or even making a sale or two. Who knows? You might even wind up with some new inventory when someone realizes that you might be interested in those boxes of old junk he or she has been meaning to clean out of the attic.

Teaming Up

Etsy Teams are another form of networking that's all about connecting with like-minded sellers with the specific goal of increasing Etsy views and sales. Etsy Teams can be based on type of inventory or the region in which the sellers live. You can join as many teams as you like, but know that most come with some sort of commitment on your part, whether it's certain actions you are supposed to engage in to promote the shops of your fellow team members or even a monetary contribution for pooled advertising and marketing opportunities. If you like the idea of working with others to help promote your shop, the team approach might work for you. But know that the time commitment can outweigh the benefits of team membership if the duties are too great.

You can find teams via the Teams section of Etsy's website, though be warned there is an almost overwhelming number of teams. Look for those that seem most suited to the sort of things you sell in your shop and whose methods of marketing appeal to you.

For new Etsy sellers, teams can be a way of getting used to the Etsy format and having some more experienced sellers there to help you in your journey. If all you are after is wisdom from more experienced sellers, though, know that Etsy's forum is probably the best place to turn to for advice and information. However, the spirit of team camaraderie can help you to launch and succeed in your Etsy adventure, and different team requirements, challenges, and goals can also help you to improve and grow your shop.

Getting Press

Are the items you sell perfect for interior decorators, both professional and amateur? Do you have a passion for vintage fashion that's reflected in all the gorgeous items in your shop? If so, it may make sense to get your shop featured in an article on one of these topics. While print magazines can be pretty tricky to break into, the blogging world can be much more approachable, and the clickable nature of blog-post links might mean it makes more marketing sense for your shop.

Approaching bloggers who write about topics that would interest the sort of people likely to buy from your shop can be as simple as sending an e-mail. Because bloggers don't draw a salary, most would probably balk at the idea of offering you free promotion for no sort of compensation. Some might be open to the idea of receiving one of your items to model in their home or model themselves if it's an article of clothing. Others might be open to the idea of doing a giveaway of one of your vintage items for their blog readers.

It will take some time to research bloggers who write about your particular topic of interest, and you'll also need to spend some time communicating with the blogger to see about featuring some of your items or your shop in an upcoming post, but if this is something that appeals to you, and especially if your shop specializes in a particular type of vintage item, it might be well worth this time investment.

What Works for You

With any sort of marketing that you do, it all comes down to what works for you. The number-one consideration is, Did the amount of time and/or money you spent on a particular marketing venture lead to an amount of sales that you were happy with? The second consideration would be whether or not you found the marketing experience enjoyable. Both of these considerations will go into determining whether or not you decide to pursue this form of marketing again in the future.

I sell thousands of dollars worth of vintage items each year on Etsy, and I don't bother with marketing my shop. Could I increase the number of items I sell by marketing? Yes, probably. Might I consider marketing ventures in the future? Maybe.

Rest assured, if you are overwhelmed with marketing or simply don't want to do it, don't worry. You can still sell plenty of items on Etsy without ever having to spend time or money on marketing.

Chapter 7
Customer Service

Something that a lot of new sellers don't even consider is customer service, but it's important to keep in mind that you are running an online store, and part of running this sort of business means providing support, answering questions, and dealing with problems. The good news is that with an Etsy store, you'll never need to hire a customer service rep or have your own customer service call center. But small sellers still need to spend time thinking about this aspect of their business, and your model should be the big companies who do have customer service reps and call centers, particularly those companies that have a reputation for top-notch customer service.

Think about your own experiences in dealing with the customer service departments at retailers, both online and otherwise. Which of those experiences left you feeling happy and satisfied? Which of those experiences were upsetting and unpleasant? Obviously, the goal is happy customers, and the right customer service policies can go a long way toward achieving this.

Returns

The idea of returns can be a bit scary for some sellers. I know that for me, when I sell an item, I don't really ever want to see it again, and probably 99 percent of the time I don't. But once in a while, a customer is dissatisfied with a purchase and asks to return an item. In your shop policies, you can lay out your return policy, and you have free reign in what you determine your return policy to be. To inspire buyer confidence, I would suggest making it clear that you do accept returns.

When you set a return policy, you can specify whether you or the customer is responsible for paying the return shipping. In most cases, you'll probably want to require the buyer to pay the return shipping, but note that if an item was damaged in transit or if it somehow arrived to the customer not in the condition in which it was described, you should cover the cost of the return shipping, regardless of what your policy states.

I know sellers are concerned about return policy abuse, especially sellers who have experience with eBay, where there seems to be a large population of crooked buyers who purchase an item, demand to return it, and then ship back an item that was not what was originally mailed to them. I don't know why eBay seems to attract this criminal element, but the good news is that so far on Etsy, I have never had an experience like this and find that Etsy customers are completely reasonable and honest in their returns and requests.

In some cases, you will find that an item that was damaged in transit will simply cost more than it's worth to have it shipped back to you, especially if the item is so damaged that it's not sellable. In this case, you will probably want to issue a refund for the purchase to the customer and let him or her know that there's no need to return the item. You can either file a shipping insurance claim or simply write off this particular sale as a loss.

I sell a lot of items on Etsy, and returns are something I hardly ever have to deal with. Taking the time to adequately describe and measure your items and being sure to note any flaws will mean that buyers know exactly what they are purchasing and that there are no surprises. You also want to make sure that items are packed securely with lots of padding and void fill to prevent damage during transit. This will also cut down on the number of claims and return requests from buyers.

Answering Questions

Etsy's messaging system, referred to as "conversations," or "convos" for short, allows anyone to send convos about particular items or general convos about your shop or shipping policies. It's a good idea to answer these convos as soon as you are able to. In our world of instant answers, folks hate having to wait awhile for a response. If you use the free Etsy Seller App on your smartphone, you can even answer these questions when you are out and about. Well, provided it's a question that you can answer on the go and not one that you'll need to take a look at a particular item of inventory to answer.

It should go without saying that you should be pleasant and courteous to customers in your replies and answer their questions to the best of your ability. Of course, sometimes buyers or potential buyers will ask questions you don't have the answer to, and it's okay to admit this in your reply.

Some of the convos you receive will be requests to purchase an item for less than your asking price. You may want to create your own policy for how you deal with such offers—for example, setting a maximum amount or percentage by which you would consider discounting an item or setting your own flat policy of selling items only for your asking price. Maybe you won't consider lower offers for items that you've only had listed for a few months. I prefer to handle any offers on an item-by-item basis and weigh a lot of factors in considering an offer, including how much I paid to purchase the item in question, how long it's been for sale, and whether the customer is also interested in purchasing other items from me. Whether accepting or refusing such offers, you still want to be kind and courteous in your reply.

The Problem Customer

They're rare on Etsy, but occasionally you'll run into a customer who tests your patience. While I'm not sure that the adage "The customer is always right" should guide your Etsy customer service policies, I think something more along the lines of "The customer is usually right" might be a better fit. This allows you leeway in dealing with the occasional trying customer.

In these difficult cases, your rule of thumb should be to be as fair and accommodating as you are able to be, while also being fair to yourself and your shop. Recognize there are some people who won't be happy no matter how much effort you make for them.

Don't allow a single experience with a problem customer to discourage you from online selling. While these experiences are upsetting, it's worth remembering that the vast majority of customers are no problem at all. So when you have one of these rare upsetting experiences, it's a good idea to take a nice deep breath, maybe even a nice walk to clear your head, and then, in the words of Taylor Swift, "shake it off" and get on with your day.

Also upsetting are the occasional trolls who decide to send you convos for seemingly no reason at all. Again, these are rare occurrences, but this is the Internet, and for some reason it does seem to attract these annoying creatures. Whether they have some hateful remark, a negative comment about your item or listing, or some other remark that does not require a response, I wouldn't worry too much about such people. In these cases, they clearly aren't interested buyers, so there's no need to respond to their convos. If you feel that a remark is especially abusive or obnoxious, or if there are repeated convos from the same individual, feel free to report them to Etsy. Otherwise, just disregard it and get on with your day. Unlike these trolls, you have better things to do with your time.

Chapter 8
Etsy Tools and Tricks

One thing I really appreciate about Etsy is how the site, as well as the way that it is managed, seems to be genuinely geared toward your having success as a seller. If you are new to Etsy, the site and selling there may seem overwhelming at first, but the Etsy community is a very welcoming one. Here's a rundown of some Etsy features that you will want to explore.

The Etsy Blog

Etsy maintains a blog, and it is chock full of useful information. The Etsy blog has a lot of tips to help sellers start their shops, grow their shops, and sell more products. It includes things such as helpful tutorials for taking better photos, reports on upcoming marketing trends—a great resource if you're unsure about tags to use in describing products—and encouraging articles about real-life Etsy shop owners. If you're new to Etsy, reading through recent blog posts will help you to get acquainted with Etsy and their way of doing things. If you have questions about how to do certain things, searching through the Etsy blog might lead you to an answer. If you have a question after reading an Etsy blog post, you can post it in a comment on the post, and an Etsy admin or another helpful Etsy user will likely give you an answer. The Etsy blog is also where you'll find any big news about the site—if they're planning to change anything or make an upgrade, if they have new rules, or even if they want to provide sellers with helpful information about postal increases.

Etsy Communications

Etsy sends periodic communications via e-mail. A lot of times, these are just links to recent posts on the Etsy blog, especially anything important that you might have missed—and the truth is, I'm so busy I no longer have time to read the Etsy blog regularly. So I appreciate these e-mails. I love reading the stories about successful Etsy sellers and usually find tips in them I can use. I also like to peruse the articles about new trends on Etsy. Not only are these posts filled with beautiful items available on Etsy, it also gives me ideas of things to look for when out sourcing or of different ways of positioning the stuff I already have.

Forums

If you have a question in need of an immediate answer, need to vent to fellow sellers, or simply want to learn about what's going on in the Etsy community, the forums are the place to go. The Etsy forums are very active, and if you post a question in the appropriate forum, you will likely receive a response pretty quickly from another seller. Of course, before posting your question, you should try searching the Etsy forums to see if someone else has already asked the same question. There are some lively discussions and heated debates that take place on the Etsy forums—sometimes a little too lively and too heated—but there is also a lot of reasonable discussion and feedback, and I've personally learned a lot by reading through posts in the Etsy forums.

One caveat about the forums: while they are a good place to go if you're just starting out and want to learn more, be careful about being sucked in to the point where you're spending more time reading and writing forum posts than you are working on setting up or growing your Etsy shop. Because one thing is definite: posting in the Etsy forums will not lead to extra sales for you as a vintage seller.

Favorites and Followers

Etsy has incorporated some social media tools into their website that help users to note the items they like as well as the shops they like. You'll notice that on each Etsy listing, there's a little clickable box with a heart. When you hit this, it will add the item to your list of "favorites." As a shopper on Etsy, I use this feature to mark things that I like but might not be ready to purchase, and then, when I'm in the mood to buy something, or perhaps if there's a holiday coming up and someone's looking for a nice present to get me, I can go back through my list of favorites to see if there's stuff that's still available and that I'm still interested in. As a seller, I also routinely favorite vintage items that I find appealing or that have a high price tag or even that I don't know much about, simply so that I can remember to be on the lookout for them when I'm out looking for inventory. When you look at the listing page for an item available on Etsy, you can see on the right-hand side how many different people on Etsy have favorited the item.

In addition to individual items, you can also favorite an entire shop, and likewise, when you're looking at a shop's page, you can see how many different people have favorited that shop. When you favorite a shop, Etsy will display new items from your favorited shops on the "Your Feed" page.

Besides favoriting shops, Etsy also allows you the option to follow other users. This doesn't mean you are literally following them around and stalking them. Etsy's simply borrowed the language that Twitter uses to describe how individuals connect with one another on their social media site. Following other users allows you to see what they are up to on the "Your Feed" page and find out about their latest items.

While favoriting and following can help you as a seller to learn from other Etsy shop owners about the sorts of items they're listing, it's also a great benefit to you as a shop owner when someone favorites your item or shop or starts following you on Etsy. The more people who favorite your items and shop and the more people who follow you, the greater the chances are that your items will be seen by interested Etsy shoppers. They might see an item they didn't know they wanted and *have* to have it.

Favorites and followers aren't something you can really seek out, though doing things such as connecting with other Etsy sellers via the forums and teams will help you to build a network on Etsy of other like-minded sellers. I've never taken any steps like this, but I receive lots of favorites and followers, and, just like Etsy traffic and Etsy sales, this is something that grows over time as you list more items.

Etsy sends e-mail notifications for any new followers. To see new item and shop favorites, go to your "Dashboard" page and click on Shop Activity. This will bring up a list of the latest users who have favorited your items and your shop.

Treasuries

The other thing you will see on the "Shop Activity" page is any treasuries your items have been included in. Anyone on Etsy can create a treasury. A treasury is a grouping of sixteen or fewer Etsy items that usually fit a certain theme, whether it is color-related or subject-matter-related. Shoppers can use the themes to browse through different Etsy items and discover products they might not have seen otherwise.

Sometimes after one of your items has been included in a treasury, you will note an uptick in the number of people who have favorited that item. The more views and the more popular the treasury is, the more favorites you will receive. When you receive a ton of favorites on a certain item in a short span of time, it's safe to assume that item has made it to Etsy's front page. Because of the traffic that page receives, it's been my experience that when an item makes it to the front page, it usually sells.

When your item has been included in a treasury by a fellow Etsy user, it's good etiquette to visit the treasury, leave a comment with a note of gratitude, and, if you would like, favorite the treasury. It also doesn't hurt to look at some of the other items included in the treasury. All these actions can help to boost the treasury in Etsy's list, leading to more people seeing it, and, maybe if you're lucky, the treasury will make it to the front page. Please note, there are a lot of treasuries created on Etsy every day, and only a small number of them ever make it to the front page.

To increase the likelihood of your item being included in an Etsy treasury, you should take the same steps you would take to increase the likelihood of your item being seen by shoppers. That is, you should take top-quality photos and use good keywords in your title, tags, and description.

You can also try creating your own treasuries. This can be fun, and it's a great way to get acquainted with Etsy and the different items that are for sale.

If you are creating your own treasuries, here are some etiquette rules to consider. You shouldn't include any of your own items in the treasury you create. This is considered bad form, and it will prevent your treasury from ever appearing on the Etsy front page. You also shouldn't include more than one item from the same shop owner. You want to spread the love, and Etsy doesn't usually select treasuries for the front page that have more than one item from the same shop owner. Although it's certainly not necessary, many folks who create treasuries send an Etsy convo to everyone they've included in the treasury with a link to let them know.

Joining teams is one way to get your items included in treasuries. Some Etsy teams encourage the creation of treasuries that include items from one or more of the team's members. This can also be a fun challenge if you want to get started in creating treasuries. The added benefit is that you'll make some new friends on Etsy in the process.

Shop Stats

I love the shop stats page that Etsy offers users. You can set your shop stats to your preferred length of time and change it at any time. It allows you to see your views, favorites, orders, and revenue in text form and graph form for set periods of time. You can also see a breakdown of traffic sources for visitors to your shop and your listings. Information is included on the search terms and the most-viewed items in your shop.

All of these are super valuable resources if you want to measure the success of your shop, see what items are working, and learn more about what is bringing visitors to your store and listings. Make an effort to review these shop stats on a regular basis so that you can see what seems to work for you in terms of increasing your total number of views.

Having this information at your fingertips is an invaluable resource in terms of deciding on how to title, describe, and tag your items. Being able to see all the different search terms that are driving traffic to your shop will give you a really good idea of what keywords are most effective.

One nice thing about shop stats that you'll be able to take advantage of after you've been selling for a while is seeing how much your traffic and sales have grown. It's fun to go back and see what sort of views you were getting in your first year on Etsy versus your current year. Of course, if you're reading this book, this probably is your first year. Take heart, and know that if you take an active interest in your shop, improving your listings and listing more items, your views and sales will increase.

Social Media Connections

Etsy has integrated social media buttons into their site. This makes it easy for other Etsy users to connect with you beyond Etsy. Currently, you can connect your Facebook, Instagram, Pinterest, and Twitter accounts to your Etsy page. These buttons allow fellow Etsy users to friend and follow you on these sites.

This integration also makes it easy for you to share your latest listings with friends and followers on these sites.

How much you share will depend on how many items you list. If you're listing a lot of items, you might not want to share them all—perhaps just pick a few of your favorites. You don't want to annoy your friends and followers with all this self-promotion. This could drive folks away who are annoyed by all the advertising. If you can, try to intersperse these shares with other meaningful content so that your social media feed doesn't look like one endless exhortation to "buy my stuff!"

Etsy Apps

Etsy has two different apps that you can add to your smartphone, and both of these can be of help to Etsy sellers. The free apps are the Etsy App and the Etsy Seller App.

The Etsy App allows you to search through everything listed for sale on Etsy and even make purchases. If you have the Etsy App on your phone, it's a good idea to check out your listings via the app, to see how well they display on a phone screen. An increasing number of website views and online purchases are taking place on mobile devices, so you want to make sure your items look as good on the little screen as they do on your computer.

The other useful function of the Etsy app comes when you are browsing through wares at a thrift store, auction, or sale. Some items you probably already know are good buys, but you're always going to come across things you haven't seen before. You can use the Etsy app to find anything similar and see what the asking price is. You might find some surprisingly valuable items this way, and you might save yourself from making some unprofitable purchases, too.

The Etsy Seller App is geared directly toward sellers, and it has lots of cool benefits. One of my favorite features is that it alerts me to each new Etsy sale I make with a little cash register ka-ching. I love hearing that sound!

The Etsy Seller App also has some practical applications. You can see a complete overview of your account and recent activity. In addition to notifications of new sales, you'll receive notifications of new convos you receive. This is great when you are out and about so that you can stay on top of your customer service and answer questions promptly. Of course, sometimes the potential buyer's question will be something you can't answer until you are near the item in question—for example, if he or she is in need of a measurement or a picture from another angle—but you can still reply with a friendly note to let him or her know that you are on the go and won't be able to provide the information until you return home. A friendly and prompt reply goes a long way toward making customers (and potential customers) happy.

I've also used the Etsy Seller App to relist items. I set daily listing/relisting goals for myself, and on those days when other commitments mean I won't be at home to use my computer, the Etsy Seller App lets me stay on top of those goals and relist on the fly, so to speak.

Third-Party Apps

Etsy does allow third-party developers to make software and applications that work with Etsy's systems to create products that can aid in marketing, financial tracking, and streamlining your Etsy store. Developers have created a whole host of apps to assist you in running your Etsy business. Some of these apps are free or have free elements, while others charge money for the services they provide. It's worth searching through the apps to see if any of them offer a service you could use. As with the Etsy forums, it's possible to get a bit lost when looking at all the different apps out there. Don't get caught in the trap of spending all your time playing with these tools when that time could probably be better spent preparing and listing your items.

If you do try out an app but ultimately don't find it useful, it's a good idea to remove the software from your computer or phone. Although it's rare, there have been cases were old apps have ended up malfunctioning and Etsy sellers have experienced unpleas-ant surprises such as their entire inventory of expired listings being relisted at one time.

Chapter 9
Business Basics

When you make the decision to open up an Etsy shop, it's important to remember that you are starting your own business, and it's time to start thinking like a business owner. Whether you decide to run your business as a part-time side hobby or turn it into a thriving source of income, you need to approach it with a business mind-set, tracking your time and expenses and making smart financial decisions to grow your business and increase your profits. However, what's nice about Etsy is that you can start out as an Etsy seller on a casual basis and test the waters to see if selling vintage items is something you enjoy and can profit from. It's fully possible to start up an Etsy store on a hobby basis only and later on take the steps and actions that will make this hobby a true work-at-home business.

If you have reached the stage in your business where you are wondering if getting a business license or registering an LLC is something worth considering, you should probably get in touch with accountants and lawyers in your area who specialize in such matters to become better acquainted with the different options available to you and the benefits of each.

Do You Need to Register Your Business?

Your plans for your Etsy shop, and the number of sales you expect to make, will determine what steps you take with your business. At least for new sellers, it makes sense to simply run your business as an individual. Since you will be receiving payments via PayPal or a direct deposit to your bank account from Etsy, you don't need to register a business name and set up a business checking account, at least at first. But down the road, depending on the direction(s) you take your business, this might become necessary. So, while you start out operating on a small scale as an individual, growth may make it necessary to register your business or at the very least set up a business checking account.

Tracking Expenses

Even if you are only running your business as an individual, you will want to keep track of your business income and expenses. A basic spreadsheet will help tremendously with this. You can choose to keep track of income and expenses monthly, quarterly, or yearly. If you are not familiar with using spreadsheets or are unsure about how to set one up, the Google Docs website offers many free spreadsheet templates that can be used for business purposes.

Tracking the income you receive is pretty easy. You simply need to note the money that Etsy deposits in your account or any funds you receive in the form of PayPal payments.

Expenses fall into a lot more categories. The most obvious expense is the cost of buying your goods. You should note any money you paid to purchase inventory for your store. Keep any receipts you receive. One thing to keep in mind is that with a lot of the buying you'll do for this business, such as from garage sales, rummage sales, and even some thrift stores, you are not likely to receive a receipt. You can create your own receipt by noting the date, total purchase price, and address on a piece of paper and saving this with your other receipts.

You should keep track of any and all mileage you log in sourcing inventory. You will be able to deduct this mileage at the standard rate when filing your taxes.

Save receipts from any meals you purchase while traveling to purchase inventory, as these too are business expenses that can be deducted.

If you lease a storage unit or other space to store inventory or work out of, this qualifies as a business expense, but even if you are using your own home, you can deduct a portion of your rent or mortgage payments based upon the total percentage of your house that's devoted to your business.

Of course, any purchases of supplies to run your business, including paper, packing material, labels, or equipment is a qualified business expense, and you should save your receipts for these purchases.

Taxes

Once you start making money from your Etsy business, Uncle Sam is going to want his cut. (Keep in mind these tips refer to sellers with the U.S. for other countries your tax rules and regulations will likely be a little different.) Officially if your net earnings from your business are $400 or more in a calendar year, then you are responsible for paying taxes on these earnings.

How much you pay in taxes is going to depend on several factors including your filing status and the different state and (if applicable) local taxes where you reside. That said if you estimate that you will owe about 30% of your earnings to the government in the form of taxes, there shouldn't be too many surprises come tax day. If anything, there might be a pleasant surprise, when you have a little bit left over after paying your share.

Although it is not mandatory, when you are self employed you can opt for paying your taxes quarterly. This means that you will make estimated payments every quarter, rather than delivering the government one big payment at tax time. Again, it's probably best to speak with an accountant or tax professional familiar with the rules for self employed individuals or businesses to determine the best route for you to take.

Whether you are making quarterly payments or one large payment, you can avoid any nasty surprises by making sure you are putting money away for taxes. Placing money in a savings account or other account is a good way to make sure these funds will be available when it comes time to pay taxes.

When you file taxes as a reselling business, you are expected to have accurate inventory information. In most cases, everything re-quired can be found in your Etsy account.

Create a System

Beyond official government require-ments and tax records, you want to have a business mind-set about all of your Etsy dealings. For this reason, tracking income and expenses on a monthly basis will provide you with a good idea of the health of your business. Schedule the time when you will work on your business, whether it is buying new inventory, creating descriptions, taking photos, or listing your items on Etsy. Set reasonable goals for your business that you can review periodically to determine what improvements or changes you should make in how you conduct your business. Your mind-set will help to set you on the path to success.

One attractive thing about starting an Etsy business is that it's something that can easily be managed by one individual without the need to hire any employees. However, down the road, depending on your business plans and how your operation grows, you may need to hire part-time employees or virtual assistants to help you run your company.

A successful Etsy business does not require employees. There are many successful Etsy shops that are still one-person operations, but others have grown their businesses and taken on employees or have found success in teaming up with friends or family members to run their stores.

For the Overwhelmed

If tracking expenses or figuring out how to file taxes terrifies you or just has you feeling confused, there is help. Accountants and tax professionals can usually provide you with answers to your questions and help you set up a system to manage your business income and expenses, but do note that their fees may be high and not something you can justify with your shop's income.

However, there are a variety of online services that are set up to help you in managing your finances. One service that I've found helpful is GoDaddy.com's bookkeeping service. One thing I like is that I can set it up to automatically import my Etsy income and Etsy fees. I do still have to manually add any other expenses, such as inventory and supplies. As an added bonus, if you sell items elsewhere online, such as on Amazon.com or eBay.com, you can link those accounts as well and see all of your online selling income in one convenient place. The service is set up to easily export tax information as well, a huge help when it comes time to pay Uncle Sam.

Chapter 10
Cleaning House and Dealing with Duds

We all make mistakes, even experienced sellers. Sometimes we buy things that simply do not sell. I'm not talking about things that don't sell the first time they're listed. That's what relisting is for. But sometimes there are items that we're still looking at years after we bought them, and we're getting kind of sick of them. If a reasonable amount of time has elapsed and your item hasn't sold, it may be time to take some sort of action.

When It's Time to Say Good-bye

First of all, for "reasonable amount of time," let's figure at least a year, and, depending on the particular item, perhaps longer. That is, I might wait a little longer on more valuable items that I'll make a nice chunk of change on when they do sell, since the listing fees are nominal compared to my return. Less expensive items, I tend to have less patience with. Of course, sometimes when space is at a premium and I'm stuck with slow-moving inventory that takes up too much room, I might be less inclined to hang onto it, no matter what its value—such as, say, a typewriter I've tripped over more times than I can count.

You might want to take a look at your listing to see if it's to blame for the lack of sales before you take action on any of your duds. First of all, check for any glaring typos in your title or description. I've found a few of these in my own listings when reviewing my information. If a keyword is misspelled, potential buyers might not be able to find your item when searching. Are your pictures clear and attractive? I know I've said this before, but on Etsy, photos can be the key to making sales, and bad ones can cost you sales. Finally, what about your item price and shipping costs? Is your item price competitive? Are there a lot of other sellers out there selling similar items for a lot less money? What are your shipping charges in relation to the item price? From time to time, I'll find myself with an item that's going to cost more to ship than what I was planning on asking for it. In such cases you might want to increase the asking price and lower your shipping charge. Then again, if the item simply isn't worth that much, this might not work, and you may be forced to accept the fact that this item simply wasn't a good investment.

Before you jettison your unsold inventory, there are a few different things you might want to consider. One strategy is to put the item on sale. You can manually drop the price of the item and perhaps add the word "sale" or "clearance" to your title, or you can use a third-party app such as Etsy on Sale, which can be configured for a certain percentage discount and uses the price-slashing style to appeal to buyers. That said, my past experience with such products is that they didn't really generate much in terms of business. You'll also want to make sure you aren't dropping prices so much that's it's not worth your time and effort to pack up and ship items when they sell.

Are there any unsold items that might work well as a set? Collections and lots of items can do well on Etsy if they are made up of things that thematically go together. Usually these are all the same type of item or, in, some cases, items that aesthetically, such as by color, work well as a set. I love old metal New Year's Eve noisemakers and occasionally will come across one here or there at a thrift store or auction, but generally these are items that don't have much value when sold individually. However, I've had success grouping such items into a lot and selling them together. Such sets are perfect for those interested in an "instant collection" as well as anyone who might want to add a special vintage touch to his or her next party. You can sell any sort of item in a set that might not be as desirable or valuable on its own, including books, figurines, or other decorative items. Group items by color or theme for best results. I tend to buy items and set them aside until I have enough of a particular sort collected, but this can also work if you have a batch of unsold items that would make a nice set.

How often you sort through your unsold inventory will depend on your own preferences. You may want to make yourself a set schedule or make it an annual event. If you're looking to make it an annual event, it makes sense to pick a slower time of the year, such as

January or February, to take stock of your inventory and get rid of the stuff that hasn't moved. Then again, if your plan is to sell your unsold stuff at a yard sale or flea market, it might make more sense to wait until it is yard sale season to clear out your unsold items.

Although sorting through unsold items can be a tedious chore, it can also be a valuable learning experience. Take note of the items that haven't sold, and whatever you do, don't buy them again. It's also worth considering what it is about the item that might have made it unappealing to buyers. Sometimes it might not be the item itself but its condition that deterred sales. If you come across an item that hasn't sold and you are still convinced it is cool and desirable, it's okay to keep it in your inventory. I know I've definitely held onto some of my favorite treasures for years, just waiting for that right buyer to come along, and usually they do.

Of course, the best part about the tedious chore of clearing out unsold inventory is that you're going to make all sorts of room on your Etsy shelves, and do you know what that means? It means it's time to go out shopping, of course, and fill your shelves with new inventory!

Have a Sale

Stores have been using clearance sales to move unsold inventory for a long, long time, and you can take advantage of this time-treasured practice of clearing out the old.

There are third-party apps, such as the popular Etsy on Sale, that take a lot of the work out of running a clearance sale and have the ability to automatically modify titles to reflect the sale discount. That said, there is a fee for using such services, and if your goal is to make some money selling off dead inventory, this may not be a worthwhile approach.

I've had better success creating a clearance section in my shop. My rule is that I mark the price down 50% for items I place in this clearance section. I add "Sale 50% Off" to the title. I start my description with something along the line of "CLEARANCE SALE—WAS $20, NOW $10." I also make sure to make one of my tags "clearance sale." It's proven to be a great way to move old inventory, and it's also a huge help in knowing when to get rid of items. If an item hasn't sold after four months in the clearance section, I decide it's time to remove it from my inventory.

By all means, if you are running a clearance sale, make sure to use your social media channels to let everyone know about it.

Host a Garage Sale

It's a little bit more work, but an in-person sale is one way to get rid of your deadweight inventory. Depending on the time of year and where you are located, a yard or garage sale can help you to free up some space on your Etsy shelves, and, while you're at it, you can get rid of any other stuff around the house that you don't use. You won't make a ton of money doing this, but you might bring in a few extra bucks to add to your picking fund. I wouldn't bother with a yard sale unless you have a lot of stuff—both old Etsy stuff and other miscellaneous items. Running sales can be a lot of hard work, and you don't want to put yourself through that for only a handful of items.

If you're located in an area not conducive to holding a garage sale, such as an apartment or a home way off the beaten track, you can try selling your items at a flea market or a similar pay-to-sell event. If there's a local event—some churches and other nonprofits hold these as fundraisers—it might be worth it to truck your stuff over there and set up a spot for a day. But keep in mind, anything you don't sell will have to get packed up and brought back home.

If you don't have that many items to get rid of, donating them is one way to quickly free up some space and help out a good cause at the same time. Thrift stores and rummage sales routinely take donations of items. Some of them might even be going back to the place where you picked them up! Make sure to find out what items are accepted by groups and organizations in your area and follow their donation rules. A lot of these organizations will provide you with a receipt, and you can claim the value of these donations on your income taxes. It's a good idea to make a list of all the items you donated with their estimated values. The IRS expects an itemized list if you plan on writing such donations off on your taxes. This is generally the most convenient way to get rid of a lot of old merchandise quickly and without having to go through so much trouble.

Donating Unsold Inventory

The one problem with unsold inventory is that it's not especially popular. So there's no guarantee that putting an item on sale or trying to sell it at a garage sale or flea market will be successful. It may make more sense, and save a lot of time, to simply donate it. The most obvious choice would be a thrift store, but you might also want to consider donating to a church or other nonprofit organization that is collecting items for a rummage sale.

Most thrift stores and charitable organizations will be glad to provide you with a receipt for your donation, and you can write it off when you do your taxes. If you are planning to go this route, you should create an itemized list of the items you are donating with their approximate value for your records. The receipt the thrift store or nonprofit organization will provide you with will likely be a generic receipt, and you can attach your itemized list to it for your records. This way, when it comes time to file your taxes, you have a dollar figure to enter for the amount of your donation. The itemized list is necessary in case you are ever audited by the IRS.

Donating your items is by far the easiest method of clearing out dead inventory, and even though it may seem as if you are throwing items away, it may make the most sense financially.

Chapter 11
Selling Beyond Etsy

Most people who are in the business of online sales didn't get their start on Etsy. eBay is probably the most popular place for individuals to resell old items online. Other sites for selling vintage stuff include Ruby Lane and Bonanza. If you're interested in selling old books, places such as Amazon, Alibris, and AbeBooks specialize in this market. Of course, you also have the option of starting your own web store, and there are a lot of premade templates and shopping-cart plugins, so you don't have to know a lot of computer programming to create your own online store. For those interested in selling treasures in person, there are different options, including starting your own store, getting a booth at a co-op store or antique mall, or selling at flea markets or vintage fairs.

eBay

Long before I started selling on Etsy, I had an eBay store and earned quite a bit of money selling both auction and fixed-price items, but I had some bad (expensively bad!) experiences with eBay that turned me off of using the site. I reluctantly started selling there again, but my past experiences and the chore of listing items on eBay, not to mention all the hassles with bidders and buyers I've experienced, make me reluctant to use the site.

eBay is a very different sort of site than Etsy and attracts a different sort of buyer. eBay has built a niche for itself of being the bargain basement of the Internet world, and buyers have come to turn to eBay when they want to purchase something cheaply. It's also a good place to pick up spare parts that you can't get anywhere else, whether it's a replacement door handle for your car or replacement beaters for your mixer. It's also built up a reputation as something of a collectibles clearing-house, so things such as Department 56 pieces or Beanie Babies might do well there.

What it doesn't seem to be is a place where high-quality vintage items go for top dollar. Of course, with eBay, like anywhere else online, you have the option of setting your price anywhere you want it to be, but be prepared for your item to remain in your inventory for a long time. Because eBay's listing fees tend to be higher, it will probably cost you more than listing on Etsy. You'll also likely receive ridiculously lowball offers from eBayers and possibly even rude or nasty messages. I really have no idea why, but for some reason eBay attracts a lot of unpleasant characters. I mean, there are a whole lot of perfectly nice ones too, but there's an unusual number of trolls.

There's no harm in listing items on both Etsy and eBay if you want to experiment and see how you do with either site, provided you stay on top of things and immediately close a listing on the other site when you do receive a sale. One thing I will say is that eBay, unlike Etsy, is much more geared toward the casual seller. If you only have a handful of items to sell, an Etsy store might not be the best fit for you. It's built around the store concept, and just as you wouldn't open a brick-and-mortar store with only twelve items in your inventory, you probably shouldn't bother with an Etsy store if you're only going to have twenty or fewer items for sale at a time. Keep in mind, it's perfectly fine to start out small as long as you have a plan to grow your inventory.

eBay does have a lot more traffic than Etsy, and it's one of the most well-known and recognized websites out there. Of course, along with that traffic are a lot more sellers. So, while there are more shoppers, there's also more competition. It seems on eBay there's always at least one seller who prices his or her items way under value, which can also have an impact on your sales if you are interested in selling things for their actual value.

eBay also has the benefit of being a place where you can sell off inventory that hasn't sold in your Etsy shop. If you're trying to move out old inventory, you can try running some eBay auctions with low starting bids, or, if it makes sense, group items together and sell them in lots.

Other Places to Sell Online

The only sites I have ever used to sell stuff online are Etsy, eBay, and Amazon, but there are other sites that offer you the opportunity to sell vintage items.

RubyLane.com bills itself as "the world's largest market for vintage and antiques." Because this is all they allow users to sell on their site, it's safe to assume that everyone who visits the site is interested in vintage items or antiques. Like Etsy and eBay, Ruby Lane charges listing fees. They also have maintenance fees based on the number of items you have for sale, and they have a one-time shop setup fee. So pricing may be a bit high if you're just starting out, but depending on what you sell, Ruby Lane might be a good way to grow your sales.

Bonanza offers a more reasonable alternative with no listing fees. It also offers the option to import listings from Etsy or eBay. That said, it's unclear how much it can deliver in terms of sales, but with no listing fees and the ability to import listings, it might be worth trying out.

Retrophoria.com is geared specifically toward vintage sellers. It also has no listing fees and offers sellers the ability to import their Etsy listings. Even less expensive is the completely free

Junkables.com, which also is devoted exclusively to vintage and antique items.

All these sites are worth checking out, but keep in mind the traffic and sales they generate may be small, and if it takes a lot of time to create and maintain listings on the sites, it simply may not be worth it.

The Used-Book World

It will probably come as no surprise that as an author, I have a certain fondness for books. That's probably why I really got started in online selling with used books. I know books and publishing very well, so I feel pretty comfortable when it comes to locating worthwhile used books. Not only are they pretty much everywhere you will go to source new inventory, but there are also many sales that are exclusively devoted to books.

Amazon has a reputation of being the sort of store that wants to go above and beyond to crush their competition, and since they started out as an online bookstore, the book market on Amazon tends to be pretty healthy. That said, in most cases Amazon book buyers are after content and usually aren't collectors. However, some vintage books, especially nonfiction ones on somewhat obscure topics, can be pretty valuable on Amazon, and since it is free to list items on Amazon, this may be something you want to look into if you are dealing with a lot of vintage books. Amazon offers sellers two different selling options. The more traditional merchant-fulfilled option works similar to Etsy or eBay, with sellers shipping purchased items directly to consumers. Their Fulfillment by Amazon (FBA, for short) program allows sellers to store their inventory in Amazon warehouses and have Amazon handle all shipping and customer service of purchased items.

Alibris and AbeBooks are both more geared toward the collectible books market, and for antiquarian books or other exceptional titles, they might be better places to sell your wares. Alibris charges sellers a reasonable annual fee to sell on their site. AbeBooks is a little more expensive, with a monthly fee for sellers. They offer a book buyback program that seems to be more geared toward newer textbooks, but it might be a way to quickly sell a valuable older book or two.

Your Own Web Store

If you're serious about building your brand, you might want to create a website where you can link to your Etsy listings, create blog posts related to your vintage treasures, or simply pull together your various social media accounts. If you're going through the trouble of creating a website, adding a store element to the page might involve only a little extra work. Having your own web store will offer you more freedom and flexibility in how you create and display your listings. Since the site is your own, any traffic you generate via search engines or links will stay on your site, and, unlike with Etsy, you won't have to worry about the wares of another Etsy seller tempting your shoppers away.

Of course, creating your own store does mean more work on your own, both in terms of creation and maintenance. It means you will have to have your own payment processing system in place. It also means you will be responsible for creating your own account with an online postage service such as Endicia or Stamps.com for printing out the shipping labels for your orders. Depending on your background and your ultimate goals, this may be something you want to try.

Etsy now offers sellers an alternative to this in the form of Pattern. When you sign up for Pattern via Etsy, it will use your Etsy shop to create a website for you. Shoppers will be able to browse and buy your wares on your website, but payment and postage services are still handled by Etsy. Though there is currently a free thirty-day trial for the Pattern website, after this users will need to pay fifteen dollars per month.

Selling Offline

The Internet has really made it easy for people to make extra cash or even a full-time living without having to leave the comfort of their homes, but some miss actual human interaction. Maybe they've always had a dream of owning their very own store. Perhaps it's just that you have the desire to sell the sort of items that are too big and heavy to ship affordably.

The boldest and most expensive move when it comes to offline selling is to open your own store. The cost to rent or purchase space, combined with maintenance and utilities, can be expensive. Depending on your hours of operation and size, you may need to hire employees. You'll also likely need to invest money in advertising your new business. All those bills can add up, but if you have the dream and the desire combined with a good location, you can make it work. It will take a lot of time and effort, but it can also turn out to be a thoroughly enjoyable experience.

That said, you may want to start off a little smaller. A booth in an antique mall will allow you to test out the waters when it comes to selling online, with a much smaller investment, both in cash and time. Co-op opportunities can be a good fit for some sellers. Find out where the nearest antique malls are located and take a look at what they have for sale and how they are set up. If nothing else, it will be fun to do some browsing! But if you like what you see and think it would be a good fit for the inventory that you have, inquire about leasing your own space in the mall.

Even if the time commitment of maintaining a store or an antique booth seems overwhelming, you can satisfy your desire for some in-person sales by participating in events with a short time commitment. Flea markets are a great way to do this, and they seem to be located just about everywhere. You might want to attend a few in your local area to get a feel for which ones seem more geared toward antique and vintage items, as these will likely attract the sort of buyers most interested in what you have to sell. Most flea markets are held regularly during the warmer times of the year, or even year round if they are inside or located in a warm-weather spot. Usually they are held on weekends, but there are also midweek flea markets. Find out what the terms are for getting a spot at your local flea market. Do you have to commit to multiple weeks? Can you select only one week or certain weeks that you would like to sell? In general, the higher the traffic at a particular flea market, the higher the fees will be, but some smaller ones may have more reasonable fees and a reputation for being more geared toward vintage and antique items.

Another in-person place to sell your wares, and one that is devoted to older stuff, is a vintage fair or an antique show. These tend to be annual events, and, depending on the size of the event, the fees might be high. Some of the larger antique shows are juried events, meaning you have to be approved to be a seller at the show and will need to submit an application, usually with photos of the types of items you plan on selling. Because these events are often held only once a year and because they are focused on older items, the shoppers who attend are usually passionate about antique and vintage items.

With flea markets and vintage or antique shows, two things you will want to keep in mind are transporting your merchandise to and from the location and the work in setting up your booth. Back in the day, this and owning their own shops were the only ways for vintage dealers to sell their goods, but the Internet means that sellers have more options. That said, if you don't mind packing up some or all of your inventory to show your goods at an in-person event, especially if it's something you'll only be doing a few times a year, then you might want to try it out.

If you decide to give offline selling in any form a try, you'll certainly make some new contacts. Be sure to have lots of business cards at the ready so that shoppers can also find you and all the treasures you sell online.

Final Thoughts

Despite the occasional fast-turnaround item that I've sold on Etsy, I would caution anyone considering opening up an Etsy store that this definitely isn't a get-rich-quick scheme. For every item that sells within hours of your listing it, there are probably three items that won't sell for months (sometimes even years!) down the line. That isn't meant to discourage you but to remind you to have realistic goals about selling on Etsy or any platform.

What I have found with Etsy is that you will get out of it what you put into it. The more time you spend curating your shop, finding beautiful vintage items, writing clear and enticing descriptions, and taking high-quality photos, the more success you will have on Etsy. Since Etsy is based around a store model, you want to make sure you have enough items in your inventory to encourage browsing by Etsy customers, which will hopefully lead to sales. If you are only able to list a few items each week, sales are going to be slow, but the more items you list and have for sale, the more you will sell, and the more money you will make.

That said, there's no need to be a full-time Etsy seller if that is not your goal. I remain a part-time Etsy seller not because of a lack of success or enjoyment in selling on Etsy, but because there are other things that I want to do. I sell elsewhere online and also spend some of my time writing books. Etsy can be a great fit for stay-at-home parents, retirees, or anyone hoping to supplement his or her full-time income.

Etsy is a moneymaking business opportunity, but it's the sort of venture that can be a lot of fun. I hope you enjoy selling vintage items on Etsy at least half as much as I do, and I wish you abundant success in this new venture!

Resources

Sourcing Inventory

Auctionzip.com. Search for auctions by location, date, and type of auction. See preview pictures and descriptions online.

GSALR.com. This free smartphone app will bring up a list of garage sales based on your current location. It's not quite as good as going through your local paper to find sales, but it comes in handy if you happen to be traveling.

TheThriftShopper.com. Search for thrift shops by zip code, see their hours, and read reviews of stores before you go.

EstateSales.net. This is a tool for finding estates sales in your area.

Useful Tools

Canva.com. This is a free online tool to create Etsy shop headers, banner images, and avatars, as well as social media cover images.

Picmonkey.com. This is a free online photo-editing tool that can be used for creating collages or resizing photos for an Etsy shop header or banner image.

Bookkeeping.Godaddy.com. This is paid software to help keep track of your selling income and expenses; it has an option to automatically import Etsy sales data.

About the Author

Alissa Grosso has run the Etsy store Planet Alissa (planetalissa.etsy.com) since 2011 and has sold over 2700 vintage items on Etsy. She makes videos about the items she's selling on Etsy and elsewhere online on the Planet Alissa YouTube channel. She's also the author of the novels *Shallow Pond*, *Ferocity Summer* and *Popular*. You can find out more about Alissa and her books at alissagrosso.com.

Made in the USA
Coppell, TX
16 November 2019